SEE & EXPLORE
LIBRARY

SPACE

·STARS·PLANETS·
·AND·SPACECRAFT·

Written by
Sue Becklake

Illustrated by
Brian Delf
Luciano Corbella

DORLING KINDERSLEY

NEW YORK

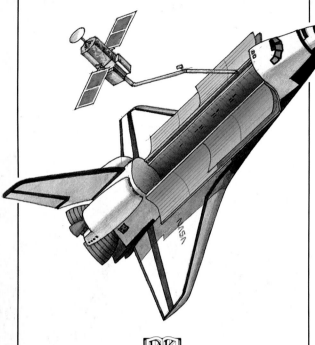

DK

A Dorling Kindersley Book

Editor Patricia Burgess
Art Editor Arthur Brown

Series Editor Angela Wilkes
Series Art Editor Roger Priddy

Editorial Director Jackie Douglas
Art Director Roger Bristow

Contributing Illustrators
Peter Dennis, Tony Roberts

First American Edition, 1991

10 9 8 7 6 5 4 3

Dorling Kindersley Inc., 232 Madison
Avenue, New York, New York 10016

ISBN 1-879431-14-9
ISBN 1-879431-29-7 (lib.bdg.)

Library of Congress Catalog Card Number 91-060144

Phototypeset by SX Composing, Essex
Reproduced in Singapore by Colourscan
Printed in Spain by Artes Graficas, Toledo S.A.
D.L.TO:440–1993

CONTENTS

SKY WATCHING

A long time ago, people watched the stars and Moon slowly moving across the sky and wondered what they were and why they moved. They gave them names and made up stories about them. They noticed that the patterns made by the stars did not change as they moved across the sky. There were five special "stars" that wandered across the star patterns. These were the planets: Mercury, Venus, Mars, Jupiter, and Saturn. Occasionally there were strange sights – stars with long tails, which frightened people who thought they were a warning that something dreadful would happen.

The first astronomers discovered that the Earth is not flat, but a round ball spinning all the time. Later they realized that the Moon circles the Earth, while the Earth and the other planets circle the Sun. They called the Earth and everything else in the sky the Universe. In this book you can read about all the things you can see in the night sky, and the fascinating discoveries that astronomers and scientists have made about the Universe.

The sky at night
Not long after the Sun sets you can see the first stars in the sky, but you will see much more when the sky is really dark. Choose a clear night and move away from street or house lights. Wear warm clothing because it is always colder on clear nights.

The Moon

Every month the Moon seems to change shape from a thin crescent to a full circle. This is because it reflects sunlight, and we cannot always see the sunlit side. When the dark side of the Moon is toward us, we cannot see it at all.

Stars and planets

A bright "star" that does not twinkle is probably a planet. Mars looks reddish and Jupiter is often the brightest star in the sky. You can find Venus shining brightly in the west just after sunset, or in the east just before sunrise.

Comets and meteors

If you see a "star" with a tail, it is a comet, but these are rarely bright enough to see with just your eyes. More often you can see shooting stars (meteors). These are small streaks of light that disappear almost at once.

Satellites

Apart from natural things in the night sky, you can also see artificial satellites. Look overhead just after sunset. A satellite looks like a point of light moving slowly across the sky like an aircraft high up.

A CLOSER LOOK AT THE NIGHT SKY

In 1609 a scientist named Galileo made a small telescope and used it to look at the stars. He was amazed at how much more he could see. He saw that the Moon was covered in craters and he found other moons circling around the planet Jupiter. He could see many more stars than anyone had ever seen before. As scientists built bigger and better telescopes that could see further into the Universe, they realized that the stars seen from Earth are all in an enormous group called a galaxy. Then far beyond this they saw other galaxies, and even further still, the mysterious quasars, which look like stars but may be young galaxies. Among the stars they saw glowing clouds of dust and gas, called nebulae, and exploding stars.

Modern telescopes work in much the same way as Galileo's. More is being learned about the Universe all the time, especially now that telescopes are being sent into space and space probes are visiting the different planets.

Seeing further
Even with binoculars, you can pick out planets, moons, and sometimes comets among the stars. With their largest telescopes, astronomers can see 3,000 times further than you can with the naked eye, and the Hubble Space Telescope can see seven times further than this.

How far can you see?
Light from the nearest star takes about four years to reach Earth, so the star is said to be four light years away. The furthest you see is the Andromeda Galaxy, 2¼ million light years away. Large telescopes can see things over 10,000 million light years away.

Using binoculars
With a pair of binoculars or a small telescope you can see craters on the Moon and Jupiter's four large moons in a line beside the planet.

Observatory telescopes
The largest telescope on
Earth has a mirror 20ft
(6m) across. With large
telescopes, astronomers
use cameras to build up a
detailed picture of faint
nebulae, or distant
galaxies and quasars.

Telescope in space
The Hubble Space
Telescope can see much
further than the largest
telescopes on the ground
because it does not have to
look through the Earth's
murky atmosphere.
Perhaps it will discover
distant planets where other
life might possibly exist.

GETTING OFF THE GROUND

When you jump in the air or throw a ball up, you and the ball always come back down to the ground again. This is because an invisible force called gravity pulls everything toward the center of the Earth. Gravity is a force that pulls two things together, but it is only strong enough to be noticed in large things like the Earth, the Sun, or the Moon. It keeps people, animals, buildings, and trees firmly in place and prevents the air from drifting off into space. However, it also makes escape from the Earth very difficult if you want to go into space. To do this you must travel very fast: 25,000mph (40,000kmh), about 20 times as fast as Concorde. If you do not want to escape completely but simply to circle the Earth, you only have to go about 12 times as fast as Concorde.

The only engines that can give a spacecraft this speed and still work in space are rockets. The jet engines used in aircraft cannot work in space because they take oxygen from the air to make their fuel burn. Rockets can work in space, where there is no air, because they carry their own supply of oxygen with them, sometimes in liquid form.

Rocket power
A rocket works in a very simple way. The fuel burning in the engine makes hot gases. These rush out of the engine nozzle, pushing the rocket forward. If you blow up a balloon and let it go so the air rushes out, it shoots forward like a rocket.

Blast-off
This Ariane rocket is taking off from the Earth to put satellites into orbit. Its four giant engines start up, blasting out hot gases. Three seconds later the rocket begins to rise. It quickly gathers speed and only two minutes later is 31 miles (50km) above the Earth.

Rocket engines
The four Ariane rocket engines have the power of 13 jumbo jet aircraft and give a speed three times faster than Concorde. The giant Saturn 5 rocket that sent astronauts to the Moon had five engines, each with the power of 32 jumbo jets.

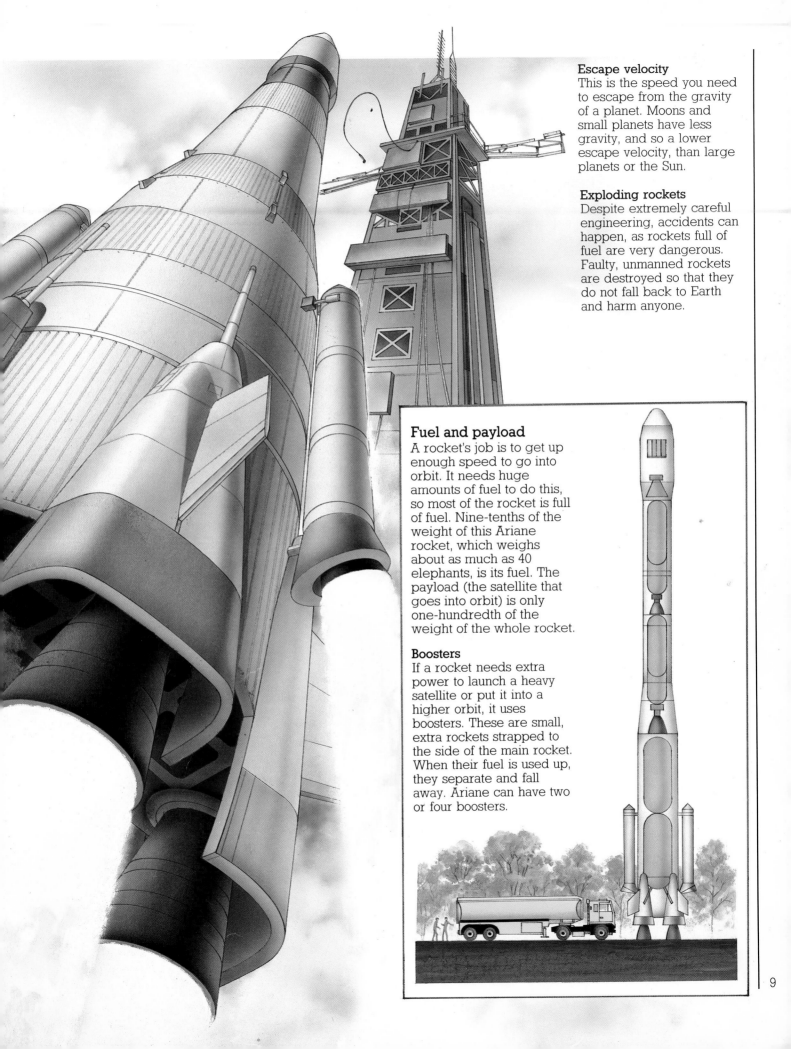

Escape velocity
This is the speed you need to escape from the gravity of a planet. Moons and small planets have less gravity, and so a lower escape velocity, than large planets or the Sun.

Exploding rockets
Despite extremely careful engineering, accidents can happen, as rockets full of fuel are very dangerous. Faulty, unmanned rockets are destroyed so that they do not fall back to Earth and harm anyone.

Fuel and payload
A rocket's job is to get up enough speed to go into orbit. It needs huge amounts of fuel to do this, so most of the rocket is full of fuel. Nine-tenths of the weight of this Ariane rocket, which weighs about as much as 40 elephants, is its fuel. The payload (the satellite that goes into orbit) is only one-hundredth of the weight of the whole rocket.

Boosters
If a rocket needs extra power to launch a heavy satellite or put it into a higher orbit, it uses boosters. These are small, extra rockets strapped to the side of the main rocket. When their fuel is used up, they separate and fall away. Ariane can have two or four boosters.

SPACE FLIGHT

Space travel is a very expensive business. Until recently, the only rockets available, such as Ariane and the giant Saturn 5, could only be used once, as they and all their equipment are completely destroyed after takeoff.

To try to make spaceflight cheaper, space engineers have built the reusable Space Shuttle. It takes off with the help of two large booster rockets. These fall back into the sea and are rescued so that they can be used again. The Shuttle's engines use fuel from a huge separate tank and this is the only part of it that cannot be reused. It goes into space with the Shuttle, then falls back into the atmosphere and burns up.

When the Shuttle returns to Earth through the atmosphere, it does not burn up because it is protected by special tiles. However, it does become glowing hot because it is moving very fast and rubbing against the air (just as when you rub your hands together very fast, they get hot).

Shuttle flight
Here you can see how the Space Shuttle takes off from Earth as a rocket, carrying astronauts and satellites into space. After about a week in space, the Shuttle comes back to Earth, landing without engine power, like a huge glider. It is then prepared for its next flight.

3 Giant fuel tank
The fuel in the huge tank that the Shuttle rides on is used up in only eight minutes, but by this time the Shuttle is already out in space.

2 Boosters
After about two minutes, when the Shuttle is 28 miles (45km) from Earth, the boosters fall off, land in the sea, and are rescued for another flight.

1 Lift-off
The Shuttle has three engines, as well as two booster rockets. Together they have the power of about 140 jumbo jets.

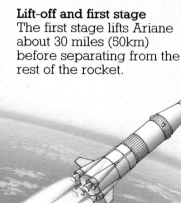

Booster

Rocket launchers
Most rockets, like Ariane, have two or three stages which are really small rockets. They each have their own engine and fuel. When its fuel is used up, the first stage drops away and lets the second stage take over and so on. In this way the rocket does not carry unnecessary weight. The empty stages fall into the sea, burn up in the atmosphere, or go into space.

Lift-off and first stage
The first stage lifts Ariane about 30 miles (50km) before separating from the rest of the rocket.

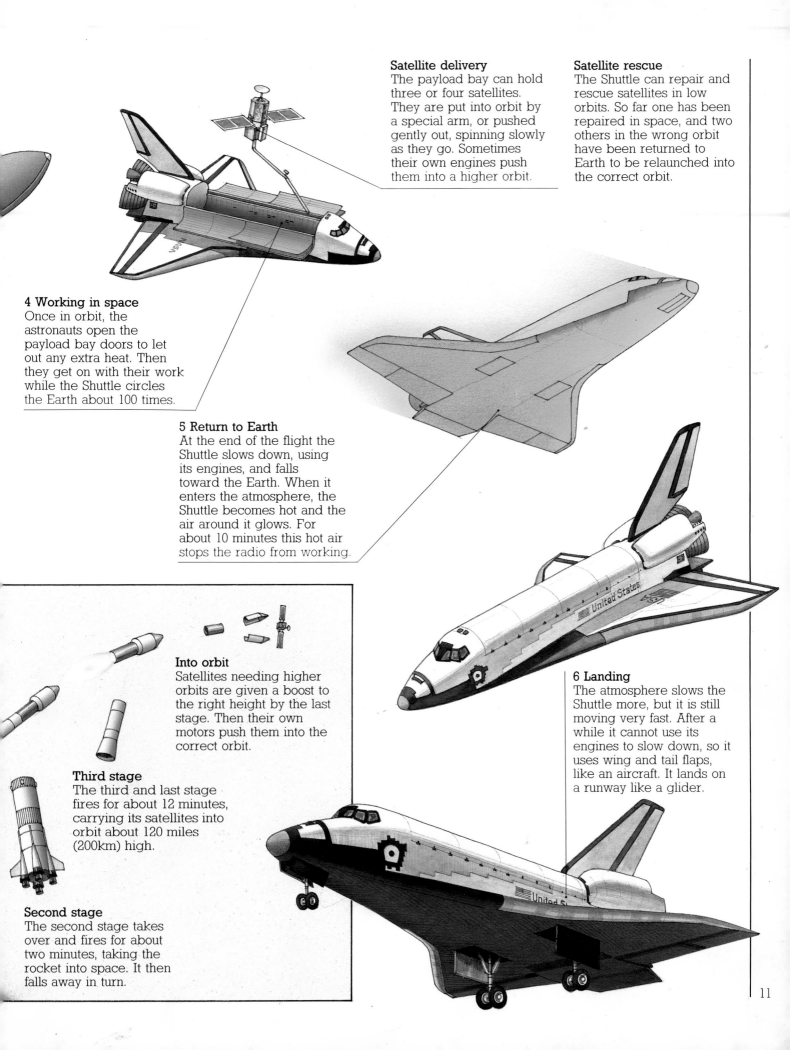

Satellite delivery
The payload bay can hold three or four satellites. They are put into orbit by a special arm, or pushed gently out, spinning slowly as they go. Sometimes their own engines push them into a higher orbit.

Satellite rescue
The Shuttle can repair and rescue satellites in low orbits. So far one has been repaired in space, and two others in the wrong orbit have been returned to Earth to be relaunched into the correct orbit.

4 Working in space
Once in orbit, the astronauts open the payload bay doors to let out any extra heat. Then they get on with their work while the Shuttle circles the Earth about 100 times.

5 Return to Earth
At the end of the flight the Shuttle slows down, using its engines, and falls toward the Earth. When it enters the atmosphere, the Shuttle becomes hot and the air around it glows. For about 10 minutes this hot air stops the radio from working.

Into orbit
Satellites needing higher orbits are given a boost to the right height by the last stage. Then their own motors push them into the correct orbit.

Third stage
The third and last stage fires for about 12 minutes, carrying its satellites into orbit about 120 miles (200km) high.

Second stage
The second stage takes over and fires for about two minutes, taking the rocket into space. It then falls away in turn.

6 Landing
The atmosphere slows the Shuttle more, but it is still moving very fast. After a while it cannot use its engines to slow down, so it uses wing and tail flaps, like an aircraft. It lands on a runway like a glider.

HOW SATELLITES WORK

A satellite is anything in space that circles
something else. The Moon is a satellite of the Earth,
but now the Earth is surrounded by manmade
satellites as well, each orbiting our planet.

The first manmade satellite, called Sputnik 1, was
launched in 1957. It was a large metal ball, 23in
(58cm) in diameter. Modern satellites come in many
different shapes and sizes. They do not have to be
streamlined like rockets because there is no air in
space for them to push against as they move. Some
are huge, spinning cylinders that can be as high as
a two-story house. Others look like boxes with
"wings" up to 50ft (15m) wide.

There are over 200 working satellites now in orbit
around the Earth, and there is a lot of space
"rubbish" – broken bits of spacecraft and space
stations. This rubbish travels so fast that even a tiny
bit of it can cause damage. Both the Space Shuttle
and the Salyut space station have already been hit
by space rubbish.

Keeping in touch

*This is a communications satellite called
Intelsat 5. It can send up to 12,250
telephone calls and two TV programs
around the world at any one time. Most
satellites have the sensors, radio aerials,
solar panels, and gas nozzles you can see
in this picture.*

Energy for work

Where do satellites get the
electricity they need to
work? Their "wings" or
body are covered with
solar cells, which change
sunlight into electricity.
Satellites need a lot of
power, so each solar panel
can be over 17ft (5m) long.

Earth

Moving around in space

A satellite turns or moves
in any direction using
clusters of nozzles.
Gas is pushed out of the
nozzles and the satellite
moves in the opposite
direction, just like a rocket
does (*see page 8*).

Sensors

Gas nozzles

Radio aerials

Heat blankets

Eyes in space

Satellites have sensors to
point them in the right
direction in space. If the
sensors do not point
directly at the Sun or a
bright star, the satellite
turns slowly until they do.

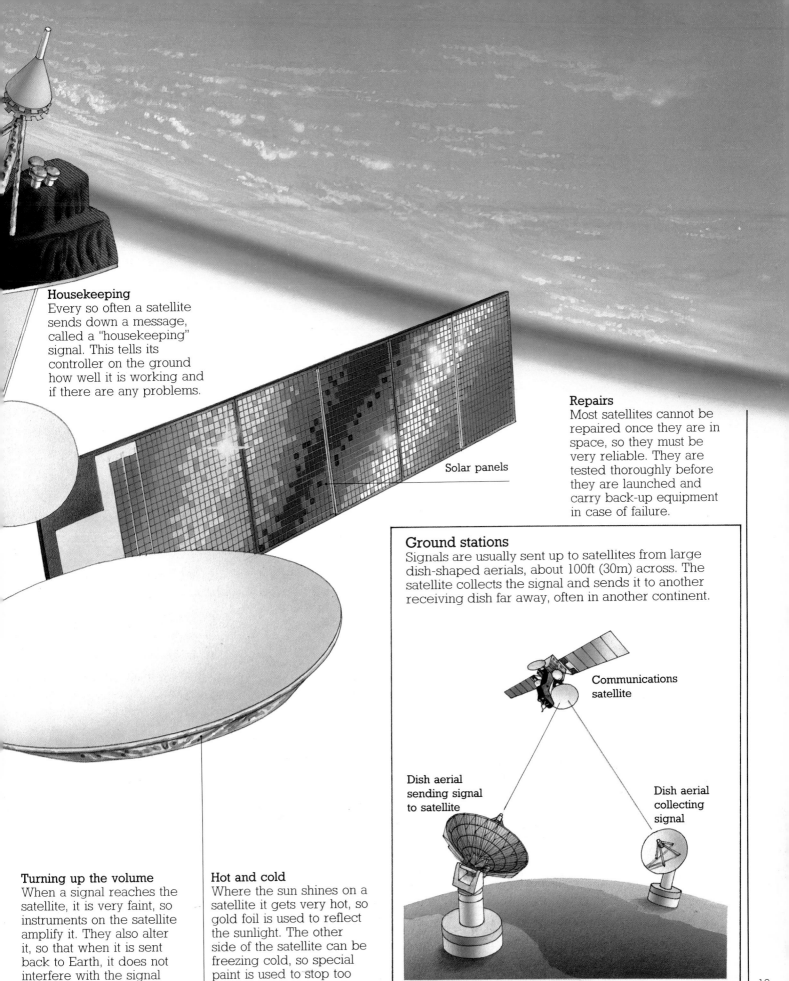

Housekeeping

Every so often a satellite sends down a message, called a "housekeeping" signal. This tells its controller on the ground how well it is working and if there are any problems.

Solar panels

Repairs

Most satellites cannot be repaired once they are in space, so they must be very reliable. They are tested thoroughly before they are launched and carry back-up equipment in case of failure.

Ground stations

Signals are usually sent up to satellites from large dish-shaped aerials, about 100ft (30m) across. The satellite collects the signal and sends it to another receiving dish far away, often in another continent.

Communications satellite

Dish aerial sending signal to satellite

Dish aerial collecting signal

Turning up the volume

When a signal reaches the satellite, it is very faint, so instruments on the satellite amplify it. They also alter it, so that when it is sent back to Earth, it does not interfere with the signal coming up.

Hot and cold

Where the sun shines on a satellite it gets very hot, so gold foil is used to reflect the sunlight. The other side of the satellite can be freezing cold, so special paint is used to stop too much heat from escaping.

WHAT SATELLITES DO

The satellites circling above the Earth have many different jobs. Apart from beaming TV programs around the world, they provide information about all sorts of things, from weather forecasts to migrating animals. Some of them have more than one job. The NOAA weather satellites carry equipment to pick up distress calls from ships or aircraft in trouble. They can alert rescue teams on the ground and help guide the rescuers to an accident. Other jobs need more than one satellite. To navigate, you need to be within radio reach of at least four satellites;

18 satellites are needed to cover the whole Earth. As well as their many peaceful uses, satellites are also used to spy on other countries. They can intercept radio messages, and can track enemy ships and aircraft using radar. Many spy satellites photograph military bases or rocket launch sites from space. They can swoop down to take pictures, then return to their orbit. Spy satellites have such powerful cameras that they are able to see a person on the ground from as far as 100 miles (60km) above the Earth.

Satellites at work
Here are four different types of satellite. Navstar *helps sailors and airmen find their way.* Landsat *observes the Earth's resources, while* NOAA *watches our weather.* IRAS *studied the Solar System and Outer Space.*

Finding your way with Navstar
If you are lost and have the right equipment, navigation satellites can help you find your way. Your radio aerial will pick up satellite signals and your computer can work out where you are.

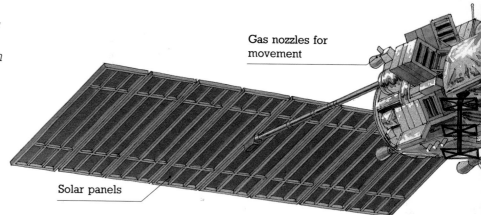

Gas nozzles for movement

Solar panels

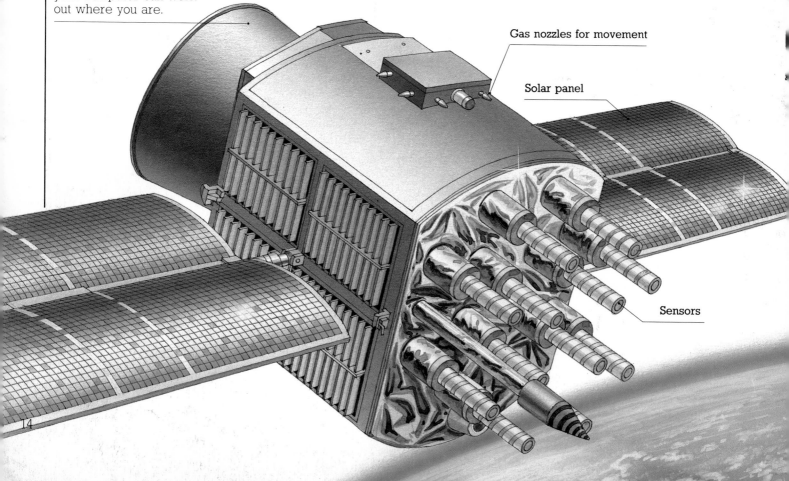

Gas nozzles for movement

Solar panel

Sensors

Watching the weather
NOAA, a weather satellite, measures air and sea temperatures, and its cloud pictures show where to expect rain. It also collects information from remote weather stations on the ground to send to forecasters.

Orbits

Low polar orbit

Eccentric orbit

Geostationary orbit

A satellite's orbit depends on its job. Communications satellites in *geostationary orbit*, about 22,000 miles (35,000km) above the equator, move eastward at the same speed as the Earth spins, so they seem to stay above a fixed spot. Satellites studying the Earth orbit in a north-south direction, about 600 miles (1,000km) high, traveling over both poles. This is called a *polar orbit*. As the Earth spins below them the satellites can see most of its surface within a day. Some communications satellites have an *eccentric orbit* – a long, thin path which swings low on one side of the Earth and high over the other.

Solar panel

Radio aerial

Sunshade

Infrared telescope

Solar panel

The Earth from Landsat
Landsat takes satellite pictures of the Earth. These help to make maps, show crop growth, drought areas, and spot forest fires. They also show atmospheric pollution, and can even help to locate oil underground.

Looking into space
The telescope of IRAS was able to view things in space that could not be seen from Earth. It found a possible solar system forming around the star Vega and spotted five comets.

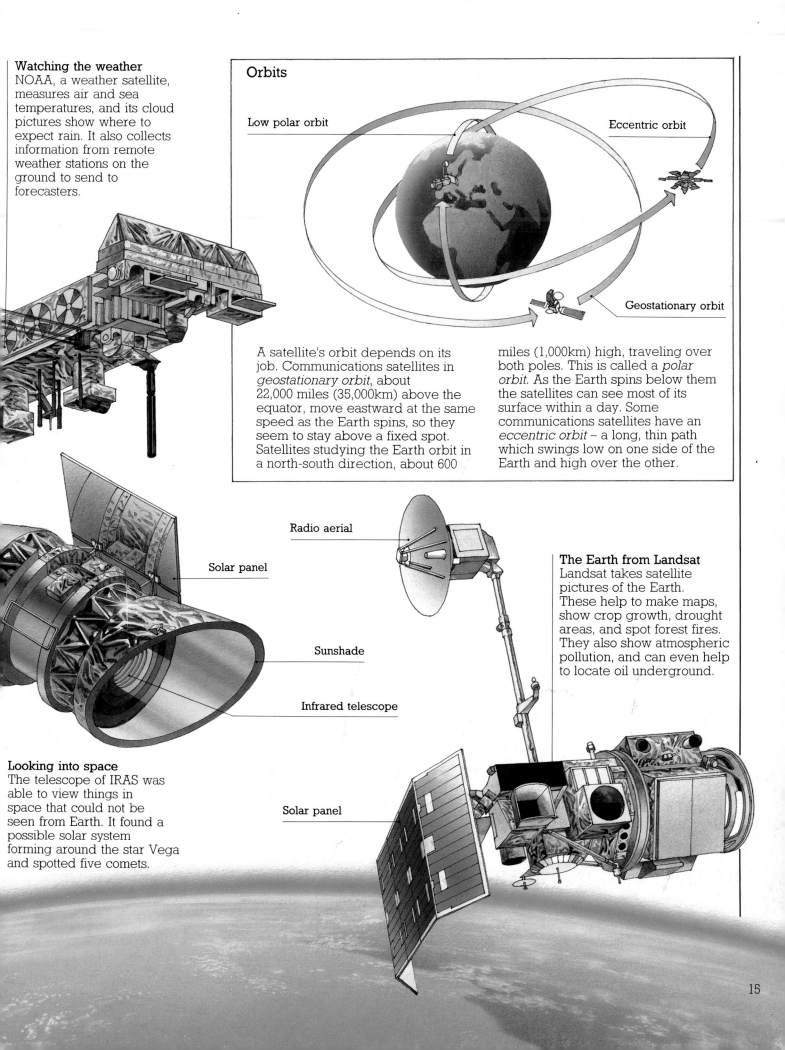

15

PLANET EARTH

The world we live on is a planet called Earth. A planet is simply a huge ball of rock, or even of liquid and gas, that circles a star. Our planet is made of rock and the star it circles is the Sun, which has nine planets (*see pages 28-31*). The Earth is the third planet from the Sun. Like the other planets, it moves around the Sun in a huge circle called an orbit, spinning all the time. Our calendar is based on these movements. A day is the time the Earth takes to spin around once, and it takes a year (365¼ days) to circle the Sun.

Although the Earth, Venus, and Mars probably all formed at the same time and from the same material, they are very different now. The Earth has oxygen in its atmosphere and is the only planet with seas. On Venus it is so hot that water would boil away immediately, and on Mars it is so cold that its water is permanently frozen in the soil or in the ice caps at its north and south poles. Water and oxygen make Earth very different from the other planets. It is the only place known to human beings where plants and animals can live.

Looking back at Earth
These astronauts from the Space Shuttle orbiting the Earth have captured a satellite to return it to Earth. One is fixed to the Space Shuttle arm to stop him drifting off into space. There has been a lot of progress since Yuri Gagarin became the first man in space in 1961.

Oceans of water
Two-thirds of the Earth are covered by huge oceans that are held in place by the pull of Earth's gravity (*see page 8*). The water is also pulled by the Moon's gravity. This is what makes the tides on the seashore.

The Earth seen from space
This is the view of Earth seen by the 21 Apollo astronauts who flew to the Moon. A visitor from space would see large areas of blue sea and white cloud. Most of the solid surface is covered by plants. All forms of life on Earth depend on water and oxygen, but these might be poisonous to a visitor from a different planet.

Inside the Earth

Scientists think the Earth formed about 4,600 million years ago. The thin outer layer, called the crust, covers the mantle, a thick layer of rock. The core is probably a solid ball of iron and is surrounded by a layer of liquid metals.

The Earth's atmosphere

Around the Earth is a thin layer of air called the atmosphere, which blocks out harmful rays from the Sun and dust particles from space. The atmosphere grows thinner as you travel further from Earth, finally becoming space.

Changing surface

The Earth's crust, the part you walk on, is made of separate pieces, called plates. These move very slowly against each other, producing mountains, valleys, volcanoes, and earthquakes, so the Earth's surface is always changing.

A giant magnet

As the Earth spins, its iron core acts like a giant magnet. This magnetism can be used to find the way with a compass. The Earth's magnetic field also traps tiny particles from the Sun in belts of radiation around the planet.

17

LIVING IN SPACE

You would be quite comfortable living in a space station or the Space Shuttle. You can wear normal clothes because the station is filled with normal air to breathe. The only real difference you would notice is weightlessness – everything, including you, would float. This is because there is no gravity in space to pull you downward. You have to be very careful to fix everything down or it will drift around. You even have to fix yourself down when you want to stay put, by using special footholds, handholds, or seatbelts.

What happens when you want a meal? Drinks do not stay in a cup; they float around as a ball of liquid, so you must drink through a straw from a plastic pack. Space food is slightly sticky so it will stay on your spoon or fork. Weightlessness also affects your body. Most astronauts are "spacesick" for the first few days. You will also look a little different because more blood than normal flows to your head, making your face look fatter. You will grow a little taller because gravity is not compressing your backbone, and your muscles will get weak because they are not needed to hold you up against the downward pull of gravity.

Space meals
You can eat normal food in space. Some is dried and needs hot or cold water added to it before you can eat it. Some is canned, like fruit, and there are nuts, candies, cookies, and bread. You eat out of the packages which you put on a tray. The trays clip on to a table and your knife, fork, and spoon are held down by magnets. The trays and cutlery are wiped clean and used again.

Packs of dried food with water added

Canned food

Tray

Drinks pack with straw

On board the Space Shuttle
Life in this Space Shuttle is like life on a space station. Eight astronauts can live in the crew cabin. Their living quarters, where they eat and sleep, are on the lower floor. All the controls are on the flight deck above.

Air supply
The air in a space station is cleaned and used again. Filters remove the carbon dioxide and water vapor that the astronauts breathe out. They also keep the air smelling fresh.

Water from electricity
On the Space Shuttle, the fuel cells that make electricity also make water. On the Mir space station the electricity comes from solar panels, so all the water must be brought up from Earth.

Space bathroom
Water will not flow without gravity, so air currents push it into and suck it out of the washbasin, which is covered. Flowing air pulls the waste materials away from your body when you use the toilet.

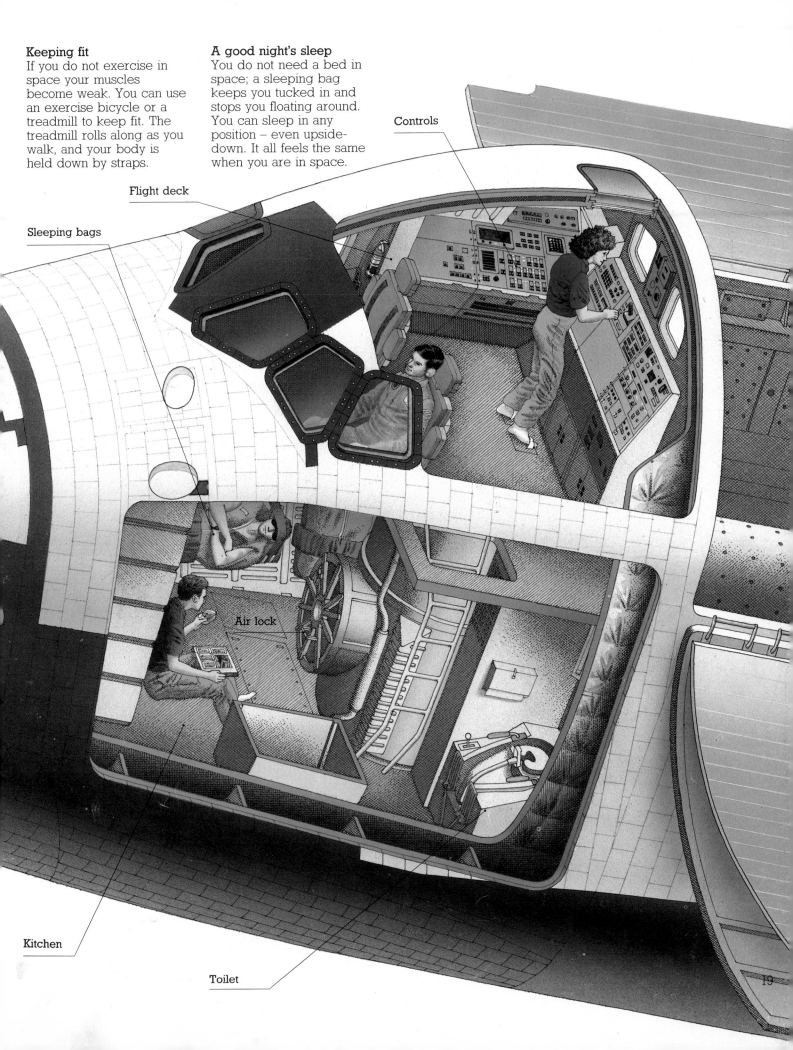

Keeping fit
If you do not exercise in space your muscles become weak. You can use an exercise bicycle or a treadmill to keep fit. The treadmill rolls along as you walk, and your body is held down by straps.

A good night's sleep
You do not need a bed in space; a sleeping bag keeps you tucked in and stops you floating around. You can sleep in any position – even upside-down. It all feels the same when you are in space.

Controls

Flight deck

Sleeping bags

Air lock

Kitchen

Toilet

19

Working in space

The Shuttle sometimes carries Spacelab, an extra cabin where scientists can conduct experiments. A tunnel connects it to the Shuttle Cabin. It includes special mounts to hold telescopes and other instruments that work out in space.

Space factory

Zero gravity can be very useful in making materials that are difficult to make on Earth. For example, alloys made by mixing molten metals stay evenly mixed in space while they harden. On Earth this is impossible – a hot liquid is never still because the warmer parts rise. In space it is easier to grow the large, pure crystals used in computers. Scientists have also managed to produce very pure medical materials for use back on Earth.

Tunnel to Spacelab

Building in space

New building techniques enable astronauts to construct things like huge aluminum beams and solar panels. These skills could be very useful in constructing space stations in the future.

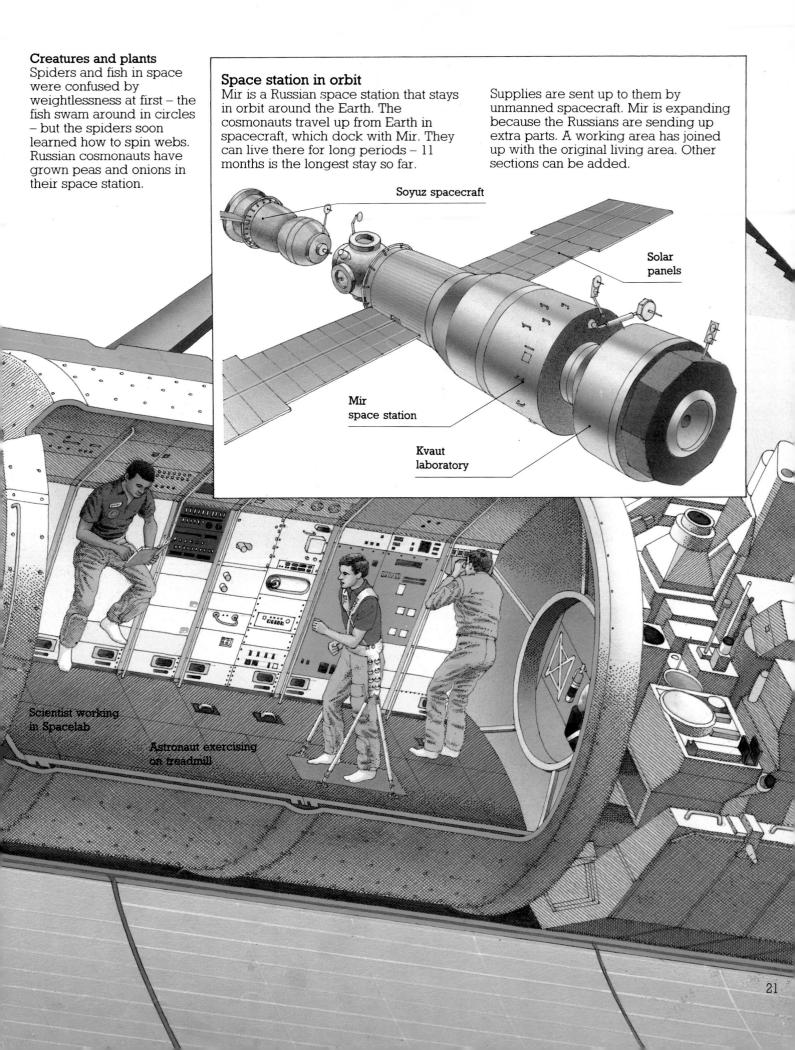

Creatures and plants

Spiders and fish in space were confused by weightlessness at first – the fish swam around in circles – but the spiders soon learned how to spin webs. Russian cosmonauts have grown peas and onions in their space station.

Space station in orbit

Mir is a Russian space station that stays in orbit around the Earth. The cosmonauts travel up from Earth in spacecraft, which dock with Mir. They can live there for long periods – 11 months is the longest stay so far.

Supplies are sent up to them by unmanned spacecraft. Mir is expanding because the Russians are sending up extra parts. A working area has joined up with the original living area. Other sections can be added.

Soyuz spacecraft

Solar panels

Mir space station

Kvaut laboratory

Scientist working in Spacelab

Astronaut exercising on treadmill

SPACE SUITS

Manned Maneuvering Unit (MMU)

Why does an astronaut need a special suit in space? Here on Earth we are surrounded by air, although we cannot see or feel it, but there is no air in space. Air provides us with the oxygen we need to breathe. It also acts as a blanket to protect us from the Sun's harmful radiation, and from tiny dust particles that speed through space. Also, it presses down all over our bodies. Without this pressure, the gases in our blood would bubble out and we would die. So the space suit, like air, provides pressure on an astronaut's body, oxygen to breathe, and protection. To do all these different things, it is very bulky; a Shuttle suit with its backpack weighs about 227lb (103kg) on Earth, although it weighs nothing in space!

Suiting up

Here is an astronaut from the Space Shuttle wearing his space suit. It is in two parts. First he puts on the pants, then he wriggles into the top half. These snap together and the gloves and helmet snap on last.

Space underwear

Although it is very cold in space, astronauts would get hot inside their space suits if their body heat could not escape. So next to their skin they wear a cooling suit with a network of tubes. Water in the tubes takes the body heat to the backpack and from there it radiates into space.

Big and bulky

The space suit itself is very thick because it is made of many layers. Inside there is a special layer to keep the right pressure on the astronaut's body. The other protective layers of material have tucks and folds in them, so that the astronaut can move his arms and legs more easily.

Cooling suit
under space suit

Layers of material
in space suit

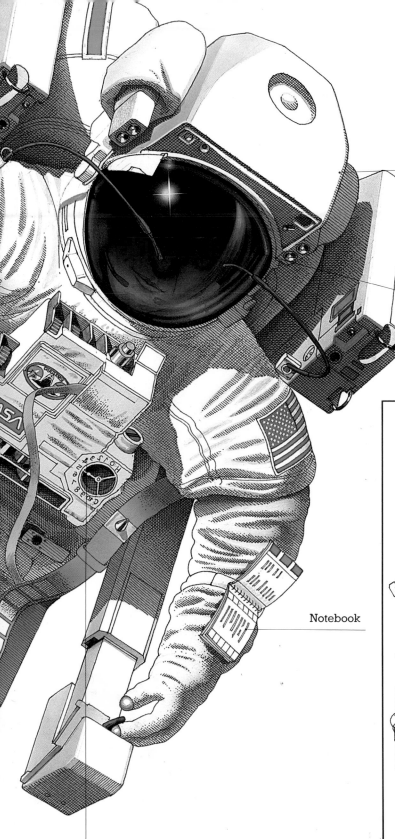

Life-supporting backpack
The astronaut carries all his supplies of oxygen and water on his back. This backpack is called the Portable Life Support System (PLSS). Its supplies will last for six hours in space – long enough to work without rest or food!

Is there anybody there?
You can see out of a space helmet, even though it has a dark visor to keep out the Sun's harmful ultraviolet rays. But you cannot speak or hear through it, so astronauts wear a special cap, with a compact microphone and headphones under the helmet.

Notebook

All systems go
While out in space, the astronaut must check that his suit is working properly. The controls are on his chest so that he can see the display panel. If he is running out of oxygen or water, or has any other problem, he will see warning lights. In the air lock on board the Shuttle there are supplies of oxygen and water.

Jetting around in space
Shuttle astronauts use a Manned Maneuvering Unit (MMU) to move around effortlessly in space. It has 24 small jets that shoot out nitrogen gas and push the astronaut along. He controls what direction he goes in with his left hand, and the right-hand control enables him to turn or twist in the three ways shown here.

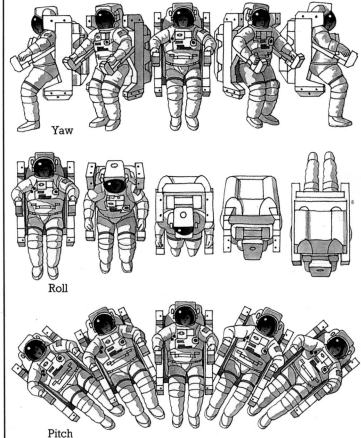

Yaw

Roll

Pitch

OUR MOON

The Moon is much nearer to Earth than anything else in space – it is over 100 times closer to us than Venus, our nearest planet – so it is the best place to start space exploration. Before astronauts could be sent to the Moon, scientists had to make sure that it would be safe for them there. From Earth they could see that there was no air or water on the Moon, but its surface could not be seen in detail and some people thought that a spacecraft would sink into soft sand when it landed. Also, no one knew anything at all about the far side of the Moon, which always faces away from the Earth.

The first spacecraft to explore the Moon were unmanned space probes. One of these was Luna 3, which flew behind the Moon in 1959. Its pictures showed the far side covered with craters, but without the large dark areas that can be seen on the side visible from Earth. Many other spacecraft followed, some crashing, some landing gently, and others orbiting the Moon. All of them sent back information showing that it was not too dangerous for astronauts to visit the Moon, although they would have to wear special space suits and take all their air, water, and food with them.

What is it like on the Moon?
In some places the Moon has high, rounded mountains, quite different from the jagged mountains on Earth. This robot explorer, called Lunokhod, rolled slowly over the dry, shady plains. It was operated by remote control from Earth, using its cameras as "eyes."

The Moon's hidden face
If you walk around somebody so that you are always facing them, you will be copying the movement of the Moon as it circles the Earth. This is why the far side of the Moon can never be seen from the Earth.

Lid with solar cells for power

Soil-testing equipment

Sun

Moon's orbit

Earth

Moon

Earth's shadow

Eclipse of the Moon
In sunlight everything casts a shadow, including the Earth. Sometimes, when the Moon is full, it passes through the Earth's shadow. This is called an eclipse. For a while it is covered by the shadow, then it moves out from the other side of it.

Craters

The craters on the Moon could have been made by volcanoes, but most astronomers now think they were made by large rocks from space crashing into it. Hot volcanic lava filled up some of the large craters, making the dark patches called "seas."

Radio aerials

Mapping the Moon

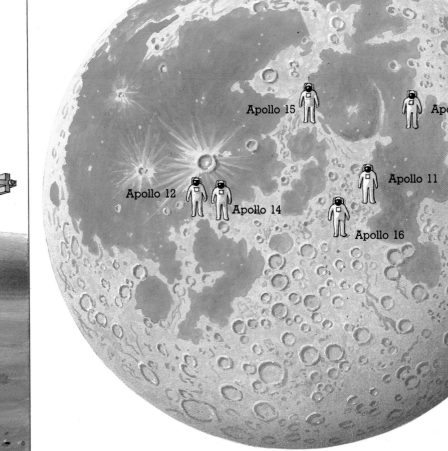

Apollo 15

Apollo 17

Apollo 12

Apollo 14

Apollo 11

Apollo 16

The first people to make maps of the Moon thought that the dark patches on its surface were seas and named them as such. It is now known that the "seas" are actually as dry as the rest of the Moon. Modern maps are made from spacecraft photographs. This one shows where all the Apollo astronauts landed.

Where did the Moon come from?

The Moon is the same age as the Earth, so some scientists think they have the same origins. Moon rocks, however, are not the same as Earth rocks, so other scientists think the Moon formed somewhere else and was captured by Earth's gravity.

PEOPLE ON THE MOON

The Moon is not an easy place to get to, and it was a difficult task to design and build a rocket and spacecraft that would take astronauts there and back safely. The giant Saturn 5 rocket was a great success. The spacecraft it carried had three parts: the Command Module that carried the three astronauts; the Service Module that, with the main engine, held the fuel and other supplies; and the Lunar Module that took two of the astronauts to the Moon's surface and back up again.

There were six trips to the Moon between 1969 and 1972. On the first visit the astronauts only spent 2½ hours on the surface of the Moon. They collected Moon rock and set up experiments. With each visit they stayed longer, and altogether they brought back nearly 840lb (380kg) of Moon rock.

It was not easy for astronauts to move about on the Moon because they had to wear bulky space suits. They found it easier to hop than to walk, and they had to use tongs or scoops to pick up rocks because they could not bend down very far. However, the space suits did not feel very heavy because the Moon's low gravity makes everything feel six times lighter than on Earth.

Exploring the Moon
On their last three trips to the Moon the Apollo astronauts took a car called the Lunar Rover with them. All their landing sites were on the near side of the Moon so they could keep in touch with Earth, but some were on plains and others in hilly areas so they could explore as much as possible.

Robot explorers
The Apollo astronauts were not the only ones to bring Moon rocks back to Earth. Three Russian spacecraft drilled soil and rock samples, put them into capsules, and returned them to Earth.

Moonquakes
Special instruments left on the Moon to detect moonquakes found only a few very weak ones. The astronauts set off small explosions, to find out about the rock near the Moon's surface.

Power source

Earth people were here!
As there is no air or water on the Moon, astronauts, footprints may remain for thousands of years. Future explorers may also find old crashed spacecraft and other rubbish.

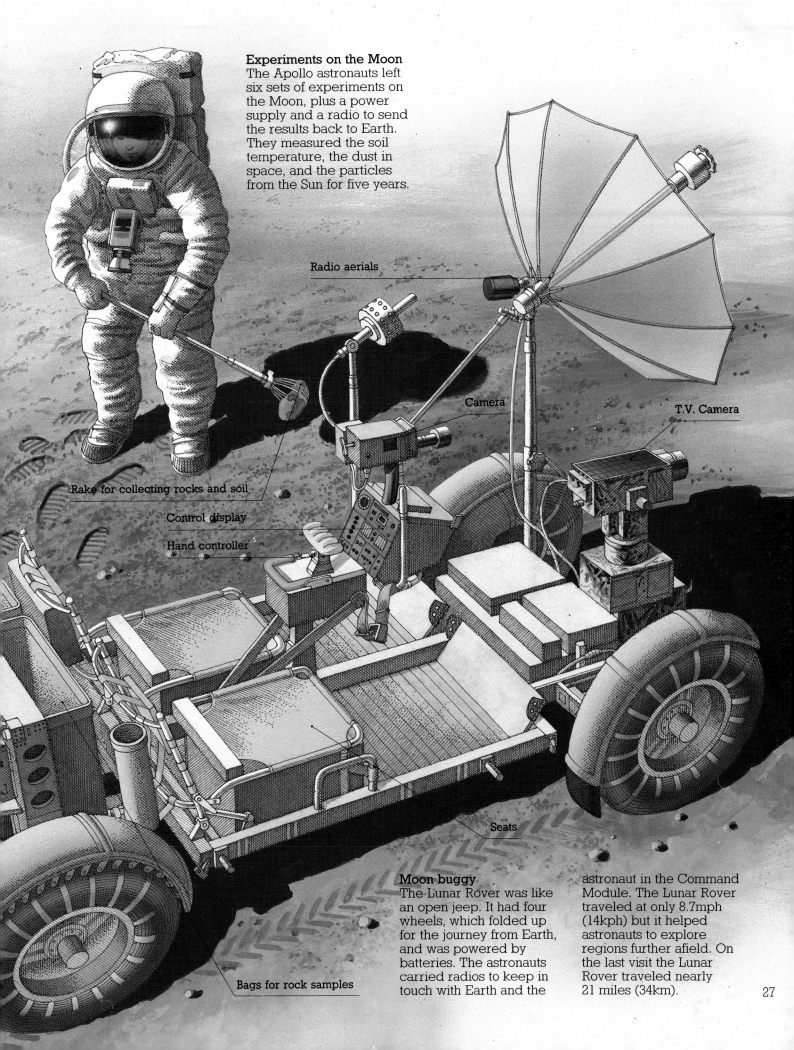

Experiments on the Moon
The Apollo astronauts left six sets of experiments on the Moon, plus a power supply and a radio to send the results back to Earth. They measured the soil temperature, the dust in space, and the particles from the Sun for five years.

Radio aerials

Camera

T.V. Camera

Rake for collecting rocks and soil

Control display

Hand controller

Seats

Bags for rock samples

Moon buggy
The Lunar Rover was like an open jeep. It had four wheels, which folded up for the journey from Earth, and was powered by batteries. The astronauts carried radios to keep in touch with Earth and the astronaut in the Command Module. The Lunar Rover traveled at only 8.7mph (14kph) but it helped astronauts to explore regions further afield. On the last visit the Lunar Rover traveled nearly 21 miles (34km).

27

OUR SOLAR SYSTEM

Around the Sun a whirling family of planets, moons, comets, and other chunks of rock is in constant motion. This family is known as the Solar System.

The Sun, the nine planets, and their moons all spin around like tops. The Earth spins around once every day, at an amazing speed of 1,035mph (1,670kph). As well as spinning, the planets all race in huge circles around the Sun. The fastest is Mercury. The planets further away from the Sun move more slowly. The Earth speeds through space at 18.5 miles (29.8km) per second – 75 times faster than Concorde. None of this movement makes us feel dizzy; we seem to stay still while everything else seems to move around us.

In between the planets are huge expanses of space. Here there are small pieces of rock and dust called meteoroids. Also, beyond the most distant planet in the solar system, Pluto, there is probably a group of comets, which occasionally swoop close to the Sun then disappear out into space far beyond Pluto again. *You can find out more about comets and meteoroids on pages 46-47.*

Planets and asteroids

Here and on page 31 you can see how the planets compare with each other and the Sun in size. In reality, of course, they are all spread out further apart in space. All the planets except Earth were named after the ancient Roman gods.

The Sun

The Sun, our nearest star, is at the center of the Solar System, holding it all together with the huge force of its gravity. The Sun is absolutely massive compared with any of the planets. *Find out more about it on pages 32-35.*

Mercury (Messenger of the Gods)

The nearest planet to the Sun is also the smallest of the four inner planets and not much larger than our Moon. It is 36 million miles (58 million km) from the Sun, and takes 88 days to orbit it. *See pages 36-37 for more on Mercury.*

Venus (Goddess of Love)

The second planet, Venus, is almost the same size as Earth. It is nearly twice as far from the Sun as Mercury – 67 million miles (108 million km), orbiting the Sun in 224 days. *You can find out more about Venus on pages 36-37.*

Earth

Our home planet is the largest of the four inner planets. It circles the sun once every year (365¼ days) at a distance of 93 million miles (150 million km). *You can find out why our planet is unique on pages 16-17.*

Mars (God of War)

This red planet is small and rocky, only about half the size of Venus and the Earth. Although its day is 24.6 hours long, nearly the same as ours, its year of 687 Earth days is almost twice as long as ours. *There is more about Mars on pages 38-39.*

The Moon

The asteroid belt
This group of tiny planets circles the Sun between Mars and Jupiter. The largest is Ceres, about 620 miles (1,000km) across, but if they were all put together, they would be smaller than our Moon. *Find out more on pages 38-39.*

Jupiter (King of the Gods)
Beyond the asteroids are four giant planets made of gases and liquids. Jupiter is the largest. It is 482 million miles (778 million km) from the Sun and takes nearly 12 years to orbit it. *Read more about Jupiter on pages 40-41.*

Moons
Orbiting most of the planets are moons. Some are as big as small planets, but many are chunks of rock just a few miles wide. The Earth only has one Moon, but Jupiter has at least 16. Mercury and Venus have no moons.

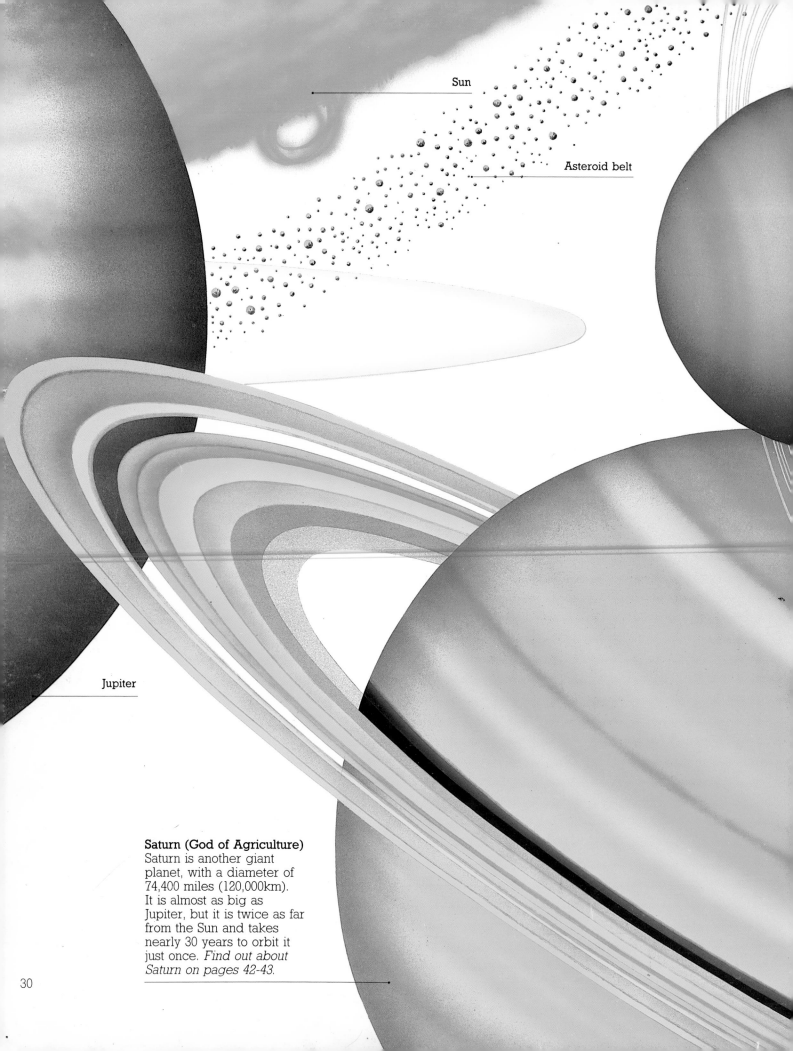

Sun

Asteroid belt

Jupiter

Saturn (God of Agriculture)
Saturn is another giant
planet, with a diameter of
74,400 miles (120,000km).
It is almost as big as
Jupiter, but it is twice as far
from the Sun and takes
nearly 30 years to orbit it
just once. *Find out about
Saturn on pages 42-43.*

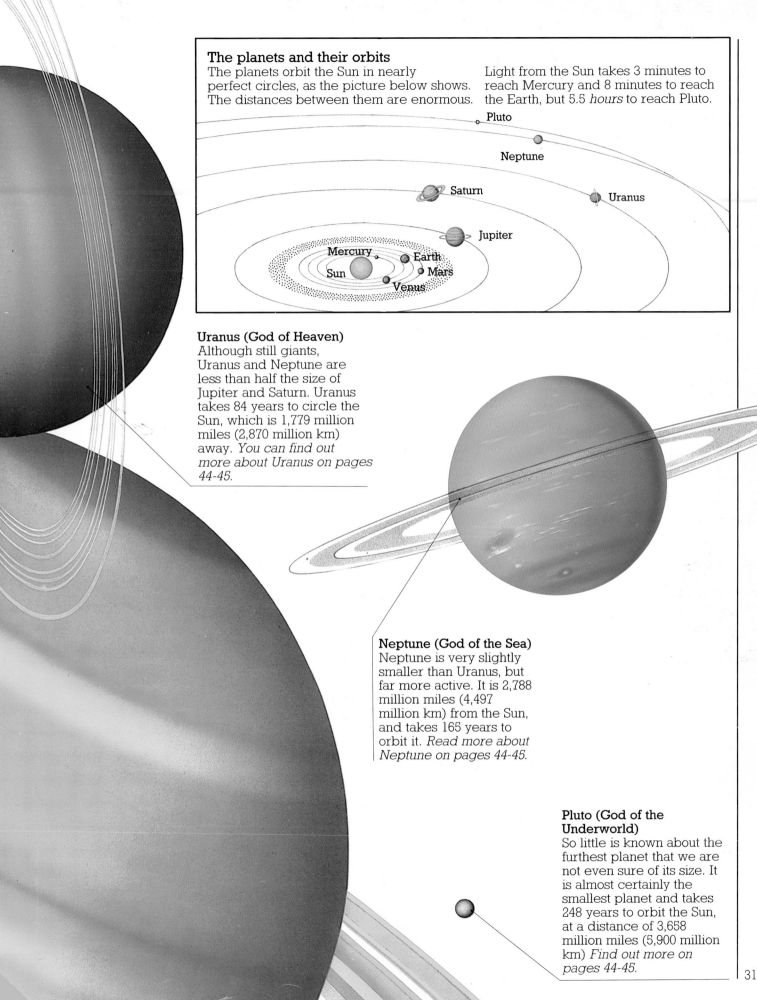

The planets and their orbits

The planets orbit the Sun in nearly perfect circles, as the picture below shows. The distances between them are enormous.

Light from the Sun takes 3 minutes to reach Mercury and 8 minutes to reach the Earth, but 5.5 *hours* to reach Pluto.

Pluto

Neptune

Saturn

Uranus

Jupiter

Mercury

Earth

Sun

Mars

Venus

Uranus (God of Heaven)

Although still giants, Uranus and Neptune are less than half the size of Jupiter and Saturn. Uranus takes 84 years to circle the Sun, which is 1,779 million miles (2,870 million km) away. *You can find out more about Uranus on pages 44-45.*

Neptune (God of the Sea)

Neptune is very slightly smaller than Uranus, but far more active. It is 2,788 million miles (4,497 million km) from the Sun, and takes 165 years to orbit it. *Read more about Neptune on pages 44-45.*

Pluto (God of the Underworld)

So little is known about the furthest planet that we are not even sure of its size. It is almost certainly the smallest planet and takes 248 years to orbit the Sun, at a distance of 3,658 million miles (5,900 million km) *Find out more on pages 44-45.*

OUR SUN

Our Sun is just an ordinary star like many others in the night sky (*see pages 48-51*), but it is very important to us. Without it the Earth would be dark and cold and nothing could live here.

The Sun is a huge, spinning ball of very hot gas, mostly hydrogen, but it does not burn like an ordinary fire. At the center of the Sun the temperature is so high and the pressure so strong that the atoms of hydrogen gas combine to make helium gas. This is what happens in a hydrogen bomb and it produces a great deal of energy. In doing this, the Sun loses 4 million tons (4,000 million kg) of material every second. However, the Sun is so huge that even at this rate it has taken 4,500 million years to use up half its hydrogen. It still has enough left, however, to keep shining steadily for another 5,000 million years.

The Sun sends out its energy as heat and light in all directions. On Earth every square yard directly facing the Sun receives more than one kilowatt of energy (the amount given out by an electric stove coil).

Huge and hot
The Sun is too huge to imagine. Its diameter is 109 times the Earth's and it takes up over a million times more space. It is also too hot to imagine. The surface we see is over 10,000°F (6,000°C) and in the center it is nearly 3,000 times hotter. Here and on pages 34-35 you can find out more about the Sun.

Solar wind
Tiny atomic particles stream in all directions from the Sun. They move at speeds faster than a bullet, but are spread out very thinly. The Pioneer probes have found that this solar wind blows even beyond the planet Neptune.

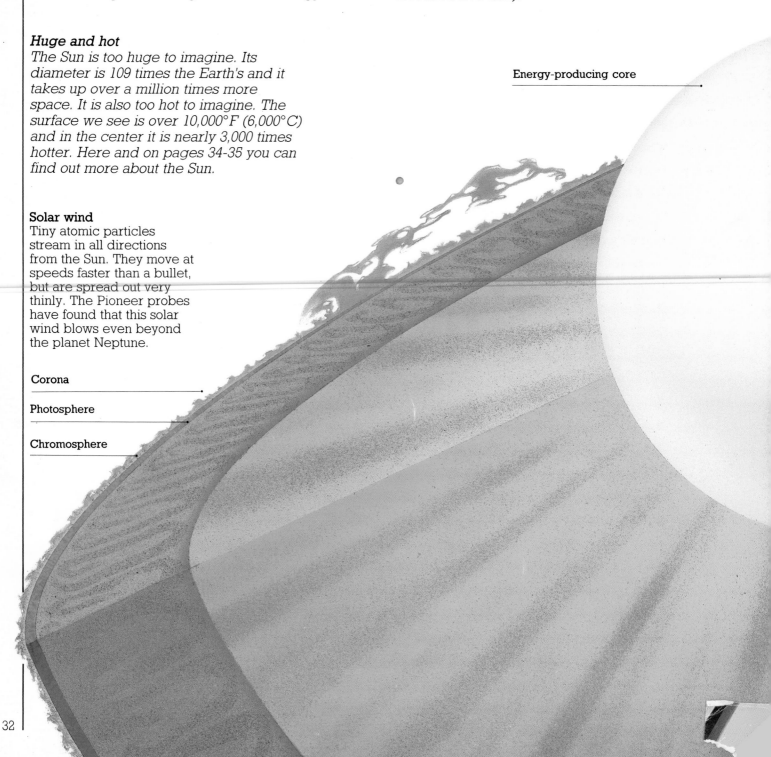

Energy-producing core

Corona

Photosphere

Chromosphere

Inside the Sun

Scientists have worked out that the Sun's energy is made in its core, at the center. It escapes outward very slowly, taking millions of years to reach the surface. In this time it changes from harmful gamma rays to the familiar heat and light. For the last part of this journey the energy is carried by the hot gases bubbling up to the surface, which is called the photosphere. The Sun's atmosphere has two layers: the chromosphere and the thin, outer corona.

Watching the Sun from home

To study the Sun safely you need a telescope, a piece of card, sticky tape, and white paper. With the lens cap on and the finderscope covered, set up the telescope so that it points at the Sun. Tape the card to the telescope and rest a sheet of paper under the eyepiece so the card casts a shadow on the paper. When you uncap the lens, an image of the Sun will be cast on to the paper.

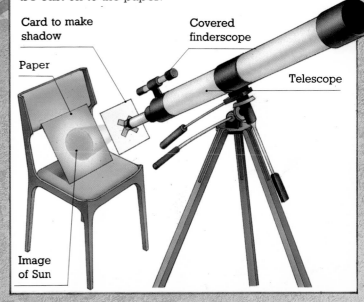

Card to make shadow

Covered finderscope

Paper

Telescope

Image of Sun

33

STUDYING THE SUN

Astronomers have developed many different ways of studying the Sun. From Earth they often observe it with instruments that split the sunlight into its separate colors, like a rainbow. Another instrument uses a huge tank of dry-cleaning liquid to collect particles called neutrinos.

As well as studying the Sun from Earth, astronomers can now observe it from closer range in space, and scientists are constantly finding out more about the Sun as satellites collect the Sun's invisible radiation that never reaches the ground.

Observing the Sun from space

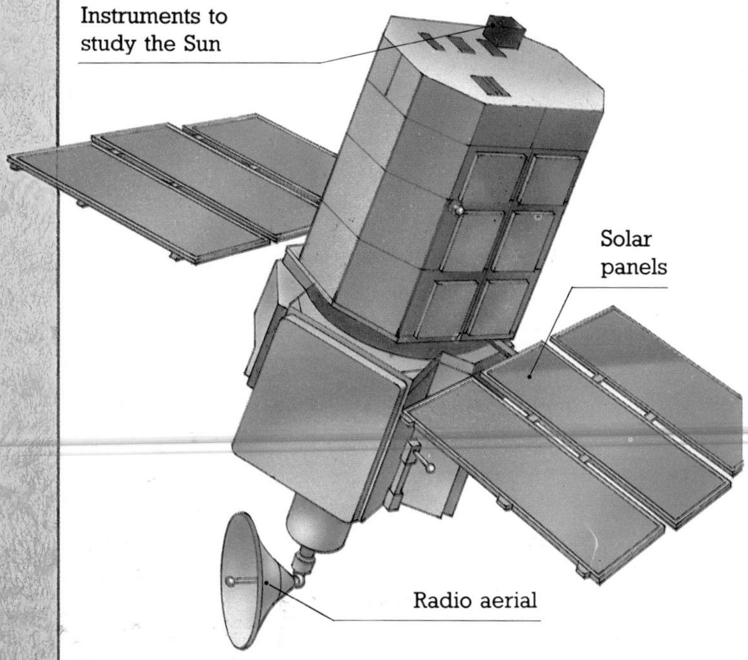

Instruments to study the Sun

Solar panels

Radio aerial

Astronomers have used many satellites to look at the Sun. This one, called Solar Max, carried cameras to study solar flares in 1980.

Earlier, in 1973 and 1974, the Skylab space station carried a whole observatory with eight telescopes just to watch the Sun. These made pictures using X rays and ultraviolet light that cannot reach the Earth's surface. They showed the Sun's atmosphere and the so-called "holes" in the corona where the solar wind escapes.

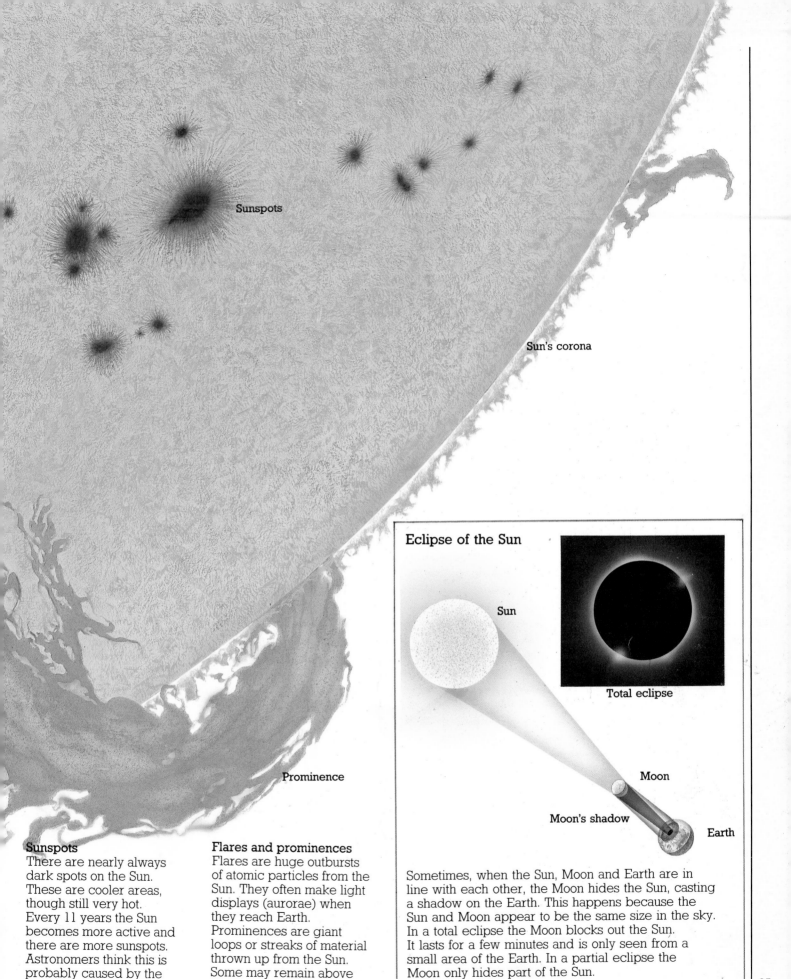

Sunspots

Sun's corona

Prominence

Eclipse of the Sun

Sun

Total eclipse

Moon

Moon's shadow

Earth

Sunspots

There are nearly always dark spots on the Sun. These are cooler areas, though still very hot. Every 11 years the Sun becomes more active and there are more sunspots. Astronomers think this is probably caused by the Sun's magnetism.

Flares and prominences

Flares are huge outbursts of atomic particles from the Sun. They often make light displays (aurorae) when they reach Earth. Prominences are giant loops or streaks of material thrown up from the Sun. Some may remain above the Sun for days.

Sometimes, when the Sun, Moon and Earth are in line with each other, the Moon hides the Sun, casting a shadow on the Earth. This happens because the Sun and Moon appear to be the same size in the sky. In a total eclipse the Moon blocks out the Sun. It lasts for a few minutes and is only seen from a small area of the Earth. In a partial eclipse the Moon only hides part of the Sun.

35

THE HOTTEST PLANETS

Traveling from Earth toward the Sun, you would only meet two other planets. First you would come to Venus, our nearest planetary neighbor. It is about the same size as the Earth, but is very unlike it. You would be unwise to land here. The thick clouds covering Venus contain drops of sulfuric acid that would burn into any approaching spacecraft. Also, as you descend toward Venus, its atmosphere presses down harder and harder, and when you reach the planet's surface, the air pressure is 90 times greater than on Earth. If this didn't crush your spacecraft, the fierce heat would soon destroy it. The surface temperature is a sizzling 932°F (500°C), making Venus the hottest planet. This is because the carbon dioxide in its atmosphere traps the Sun's heat, like glass in a greenhouse.

As you leave Venus and continue toward the Sun you would meet Mercury, the closest planet to the Sun. Mercury takes 59 days to spin once and has very long days and nights. This means that it is very hot on the side facing the Sun, but extremely cold on the dark side of the planet, especially as there is no atmosphere to trap the heat from the Sun.

Exploring Venus and Mercury
It took this space probe, Mariner 10, 52 days to speed across the vast distance between Venus and Mercury. It found two very different planets: Venus shrouded in clouds and Mercury, a hot, dry, airless ball of rock.

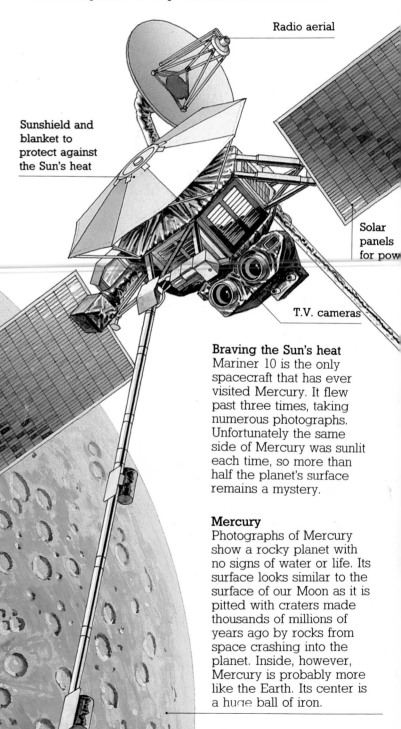

Radio aerial

Sunshield and blanket to protect against the Sun's heat

Solar panels for pow[er]

T.V. cameras

Braving the Sun's heat
Mariner 10 is the only spacecraft that has ever visited Mercury. It flew past three times, taking numerous photographs. Unfortunately the same side of Mercury was sunlit each time, so more than half the planet's surface remains a mystery.

Mercury
Photographs of Mercury show a rocky planet with no signs of water or life. Its surface looks similar to the surface of our Moon as it is pitted with craters made thousands of millions of years ago by rocks from space crashing into the planet. Inside, however, Mercury is probably more like the Earth. Its center is a huge ball of iron.

Venus

Mariner 10 also photographed Venus's clouds, which race around the planet in four days. Venus itself takes 243 Earth days to spin once. It only takes 225 Earth days to orbit the Sun, so its day is longer than its year. Venus also spins in the opposite direction to all the other planets. Orbiting spacecraft have now mapped most of its surface using radar.

Surviving on Venus

Several Russian Venera spacecraft have landed on Venus and survived long enough to send back pictures. They even tested some of the reddish-brown rocks. Beneath the clouds they found a bright orange sky. They also saw flashes of lightning, which could mean that there are active volcanoes on Venus.

MARS AND THE ASTEROID BELT

There was a time when many people thought that visitors to Mars would meet intelligent Martians. However, the first exploring spacecraft saw no signs of life as it flew past the dry, rocky planet. When the Viking robot explorers landed on the surface and searched the soil for tiny living creatures, they also found nothing definite. Although there seems to be no life there now, Mars is probably the best place in the Solar System for people to set up a base. It is like the Earth in some ways. Its day is about the same length as ours and it has summer and winter seasons, though its year is twice as long as ours.

Life would not be easy on Mars. There is no running water and it is very cold because it is a lot further from the Sun than the Earth. Its thin atmosphere is made of carbon dioxide, so we could not breathe it and it doesn't block out the Sun's harmful radiation like the Earth's atmosphere. The journey from Earth would take a long time. At their closest, Mars and Earth are 34 million miles (55 million km) apart but they only come this close once every 16 years. The Viking spacecraft took nearly a year to get there and radio messages took almost 20 minutes to get back to Earth.

Rusty red rocks

Mars is sometimes called the Red Planet because the soil and rocks are red. Its dusty plains are littered with rocks and scarred by canyons and extinct volcanoes. Although Mars is lifeless now, it once had rivers. Perhaps one day we may find some fossilized signs of life.

Viking visitors

When the Viking spacecraft arrived to explore Mars, the Landers parachuted down to the surface. The Orbiters circled the planet, mapping the surface, measuring the temperatures, and watching the ice caps.

Viking on Mars

Two of these Viking spacecraft landed on Mars in 1976. They photographed the landscape and recorded the weather, winds, and temperatures. They also listened for Martian earthquakes. The soil samples they tested did not seem to contain life.

Earth (Mars) quake detector

Radio aerial

Cameras

Engine for landing

Sample tester

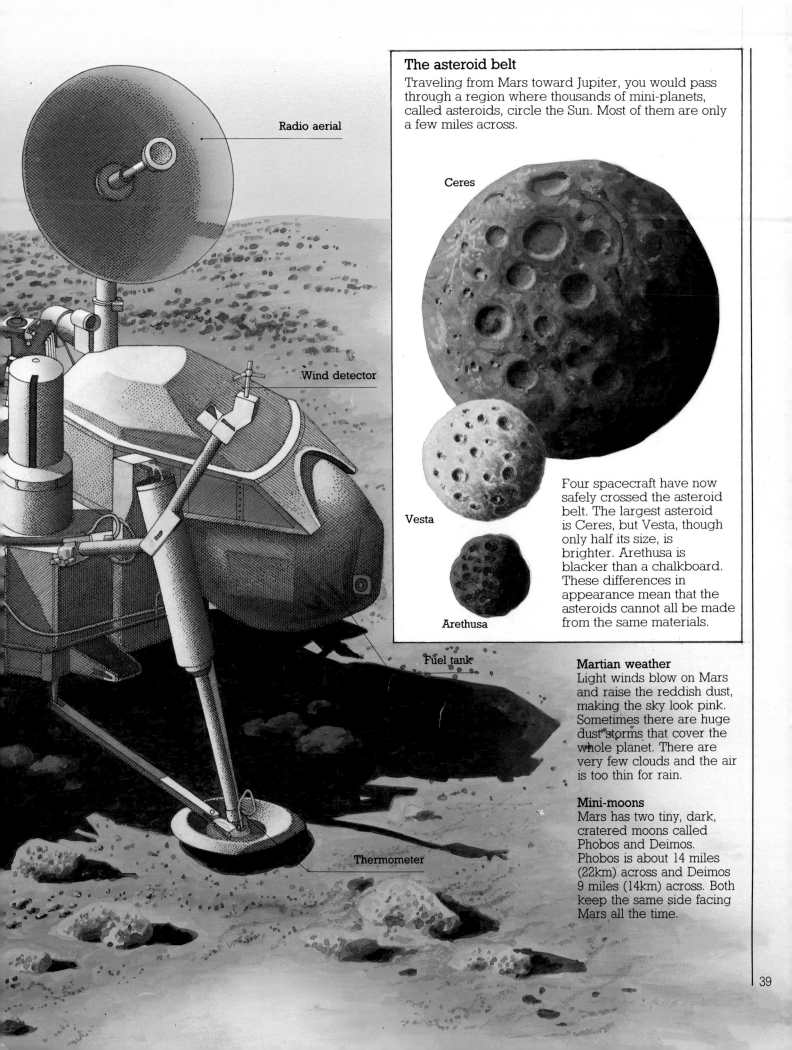

Radio aerial

Wind detector

Fuel tank

Thermometer

The asteroid belt

Traveling from Mars toward Jupiter, you would pass through a region where thousands of mini-planets, called asteroids, circle the Sun. Most of them are only a few miles across.

Ceres

Vesta

Arethusa

Four spacecraft have now safely crossed the asteroid belt. The largest asteroid is Ceres, but Vesta, though only half its size, is brighter. Arethusa is blacker than a chalkboard. These differences in appearance mean that the asteroids cannot all be made from the same materials.

Martian weather
Light winds blow on Mars and raise the reddish dust, making the sky look pink. Sometimes there are huge dust storms that cover the whole planet. There are very few clouds and the air is too thin for rain.

Mini-moons
Mars has two tiny, dark, cratered moons called Phobos and Deimos. Phobos is about 14 miles (22km) across and Deimos 9 miles (14km) across. Both keep the same side facing Mars all the time.

JUPITER

Once through the asteroid belt, an exploring spacecraft would meet Jupiter, the largest planet in the Solar System. All the other planets put together could fit into it twice over and the Earth on its own would fit into it over 1,318 times.

Jupiter is a dangerous place. It acts like a powerful magnet and traps radiation from the Sun that forms belts around the planet. This radiation is 100,000 times stronger than the amount needed to kill a human. It would be impossible to land on Jupiter in any case because it is a huge ball of liquid. The surface of the liquid is covered with clouds, and as you go down through them, the gas in Jupiter's atmosphere, mainly hydrogen, presses down harder and harder until it is so condensed that it becomes liquid. At the center of the planet, astronomers think there is a solid ball of rock about the same size as the Earth.

How does this huge liquid planet hold its shape? It is held together by gravity, but it does bulge out around its equator because it spins very fast, taking only about 10 hours to turn once. Around the equator is a narrow ring of dark, dusty material that is invisible from Earth, but can be seen from passing spacecraft.

Flying past Jupiter

Pioneer 10 flew past Jupiter in 1973, passing through the dangerous radiation belts, which interfered with some of its instruments. It then flew out of the Solar System toward the stars, and by 1983 was beyond the furthest known planet.

Swirling patterns

Jupiter's clouds are icy cold. Powerful winds blow them into striped patterns. The bright bands are formed by higher clouds and the dark bands by lower clouds.

The Great Red Spot

For 300 years astronomers have been studying a mysterious giant red spot on Jupiter. Sometimes it disappears but it always returns. It is a huge column of whirling clouds.

Galileo

The next spacecraft to Jupiter will study its surface, its moons, and its atmosphere. A small probe will drop into the clouds, examine them, and take their temperatures.

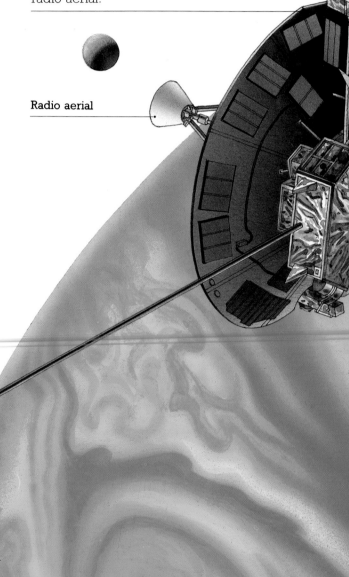

The Pioneers
Pioneers 10 and 11 proved that it was possible to travel safely through the asteroid belt to the giant planets. They sent back lots of information on Jupiter using a large dish radio aerial.

Radio aerial

Instrument to measure Jupiter's magnetism

Power supplies

Asteroid detector

The moons of Jupiter

Jupiter has 16 moons. Twelve of them are very small, but four of them (discovered by Galileo in 1610) are the size of planets. The largest of them, Ganymede, is larger than Mercury. Three of the small moons were discovered by Voyager (in 1979 and 1980).

Europa

Io

When the Voyager spacecraft flew past Io, scientists saw erupting volcanoes. These throw out millions of tons of material every year, so the surface of Io is constantly changing.

Io

Ganymede

Callisto

Europa, Ganymede, and Callisto

These moons are covered in ice. Europa has a white surface, while Ganymede has dark areas with craters. Callisto, outside the radiation belts, is covered in craters.

SATURN

Traveling out beyond Jupiter, twice as far from the Sun, you come to Saturn, a huge liquid planet with a small, solid center. Because Saturn is a spinning ball of liquid, it bulges at the equator. It is also very light. If you had a large enough bucket, it would be able to float on water.

Orbiting Saturn, you would look down on the clouds that hide it. These clouds are not as colorful as Jupiter's because they have a layer of haze above them, but they move faster. They are also very cold because Saturn is so far from the Sun. The Earth receives about 100 times more heat from the Sun than Saturn does.

As you cannot land on Saturn, you would probably land on one of its many rocky moons. Titan, the largest, is the only moon in the Solar System with an atmosphere and clouds. Saturn's main attraction is the fabulous set of rings around its equator. The rings are really thousands of ringlets made of millions of glittering icy particles.

Exploring planets, moons, and rings
This Voyager spacecraft is flying past the large moon, Titan, on its way to explore Saturn. Voyagers 1 and 2 took nearly three years to reach Saturn. They took close-up photographs of the planet, its rings, and its known moons as they passed by.

T.V. camera

Voyaging to the planets
Two Voyager spacecraft reached Jupiter in 1979. In 1980 and 1981 they passed Saturn, where they discovered 11 previously unknown moons. Voyager 2 passed Uranus in 1986 and Neptune in 1989.

Radio aerial pointing toward Earth

Messages for the stars
The Pioneer and Voyager spacecraft carry messages for anyone they may meet in space. Voyagers 1 and 2 each carry a record of Earth sounds, for an alien with a record player!

Fuel tank

Power supply

Titan
Saturn's largest moon may not be the best one to land on. Its freezing atmosphere is made of nitrogen and methane, which we cannot breathe. Methane seas and rain may be present on Titan.

What are the rings made of?

Saturn's rings are made of millions of bits of ice. These range from tiny particles to lumps 7 miles (10km) across. They circle Saturn in a thin disc and the main rings measure about as much across as the distance from the Moon to the Earth.

Iceberg moons
Saturn has six medium-sized moons. They look a bit like our Moon, with craters, valleys, and ridges, but they are all very cold – probably made almost entirely of ice.

Rings and moons
Circling among the rings and large moons are 14 tiny moons, some only 19 miles (30km) across. Small moons on either side of a ring are called "shepherd moons."

DISCOVERING THE OUTER PLANETS

All the planets out as far as Saturn were well known to ancient astronomers because they shine brightly in the sky. Uranus was discovered by accident in 1781, when William Herschel mistook it for a comet. Other astronomers later realized that he had found a new planet, but Uranus did not follow its expected path around the Sun. There had to be another unknown planet pulling it off course. Neptune was discovered in 1847, just where this new planet should be. Neptune also seemed to be moving off course, but it was not until 1930 that astronomers eventually found Pluto.

However, this may not be the end of the story. Pluto was much smaller than anyone expected and some astronomers have suggested that there may be yet another planet beyond it. They will be tracking the Pioneer and Voyager spacecraft to see if they are pulled off course by an unknown planet.

Astronomers are still making exciting discoveries about these far planets. In 1977 they were watching Uranus move in front of a distant star and saw the star "blink" on and off several times on either side of the planet. They had discovered a set of rings around Uranus. In 1978 they discovered that Pluto had a moon, and called it Charon.

Flying past Uranus

When Voyager 2 flew past Uranus in 1986 it had been traveling through space for nine years. It discovered 10 more moons and another ring around the planet, making 15 moons and 10 rings altogether. It also sent back close-ups of the five larger moons, the rings, and the planet itself.

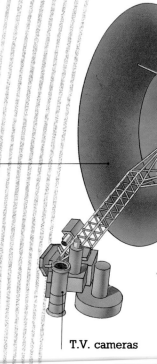

Radio aerial pointing at Earth

Voyaging to the planets

The outer planets are in line for visiting spacecraft only once every 175 years. Between 1979 and 1989 Jupiter, Saturn, Uranus, and Neptune were all on the same side of the Sun, so Voyager could swing past each planet in turn.

T.V. cameras

A smaller gas giant

Uranus, greenish and very cold, seems to be mostly liquid and gas like Jupiter and Saturn, but it is only about half their size and does not have cloud patterns. Its 15 moons are all smaller than our Moon and icy cold.

Uranus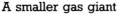

The tilted planet

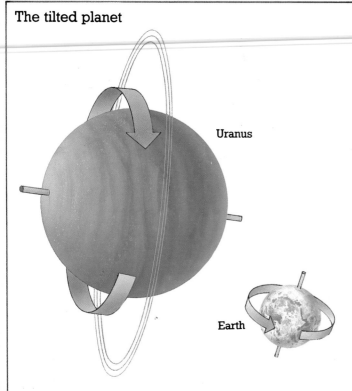

Uranus

Earth

Uranus looks as if it is spinning on its side. As it moves around the Sun, sunlight falls for periods of 21 Earth years first on one pole, then on the equator, and then on the other pole. This creates very odd seasons, as each pole has 21 years of sunlight followed by 21 years of normal days and nights, and then 21 years of darkness.

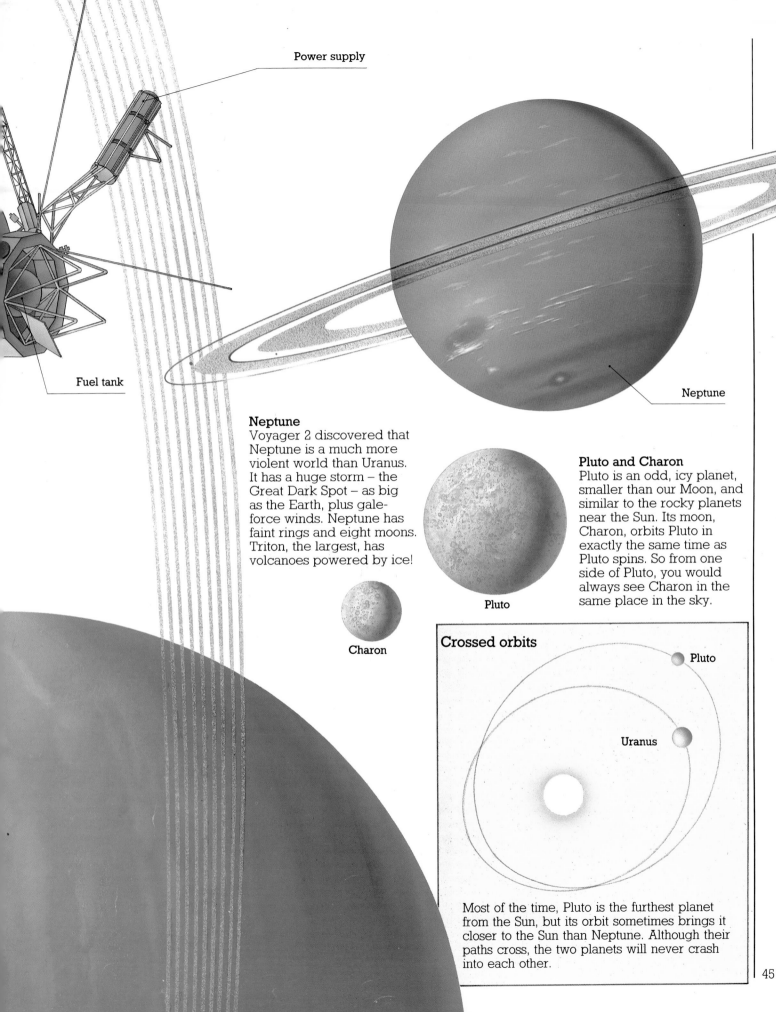

Power supply

Fuel tank

Neptune

Neptune
Voyager 2 discovered that
Neptune is a much more
violent world than Uranus.
It has a huge storm – the
Great Dark Spot – as big
as the Earth, plus gale-
force winds. Neptune has
faint rings and eight moons.
Triton, the largest, has
volcanoes powered by ice!

Pluto

Charon

Pluto and Charon
Pluto is an odd, icy planet,
smaller than our Moon, and
similar to the rocky planets
near the Sun. Its moon,
Charon, orbits Pluto in
exactly the same time as
Pluto spins. So from one
side of Pluto, you would
always see Charon in the
same place in the sky.

Crossed orbits

Pluto

Uranus

Most of the time, Pluto is the furthest planet
from the Sun, but its orbit sometimes brings it
closer to the Sun than Neptune. Although their
paths cross, the two planets will never crash
into each other.

45

COMETS AND METEORS

Comets are strange but beautiful sights, like stars with long tails. They appear in the sky without warning and are sometimes very large and bright. Long ago people thought they were a dreadful warning of death or disaster. Now we know that the comet itself, the nucleus, is so small that it cannot even be seen from Earth. It is made of ice and dust, like a dirty snowball. When it comes near the Sun, the heat makes a cloud of dust and gas around the nucleus. This is called the coma and the solar wind blows it out into an enormous tail. The gas glows and the dust reflects sunlight, making the glorious sight we see from Earth. Sometimes comets have two tails, a thin straight tail of gas and a wider, spread-out tail of dust.

Astronomers think that the Solar System may be surrounded by a cloud of comets far beyond the furthest planet. It is only when a comet leaves this cloud and swings very close to the Sun that it can be seen from Earth.

Coming or going?
Comet tails can be millions of miles long. As they always point away from the Sun, comets sometimes travel tail first. They contain little material, so the Earth can pass through one without harm.

Visitors for Halley's Comet
This European space probe, called Giotto, was one of five that went out to meet Halley's Comet in 1986. Its pictures showed a potato-shaped nucleus only about 9 miles (15km) long and 5 miles (8km) wide.

Giotto
Giotto flew through the cloud of dust and gas around Halley's comet. In spite of its protective dust shield, the spacecraft was damaged, but it sent back pictures of the nucleus, which was losing 15 tons (15,000kg) of gas every second.

Halley's Comet
Some comets return to the Sun regularly. The most famous is Halley's Comet, last seen in 1986. It comes back every 76 years, and has been observed for over 2,000 years.

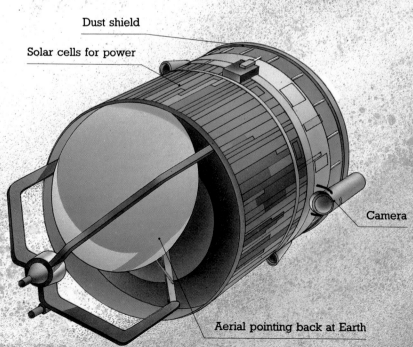

Dust shield

Solar cells for power

Camera

Aerial pointing back at Earth

Nucleus

Shooting stars

Shooting stars, or meteors, are streaks of light made by space dust, with particles the size of grains of sand, burning up as it enters the Earth's atmosphere. Larger pieces that crash down to Earth are called meteorites and they sometimes make craters. A crater in Arizona is 3,937 ft (1,200 m) across and probably as much as 24,000 years old.

THE LIFE AND DEATH OF A STAR

On a clear night you can see that the stars are not all the same. Some look brighter than others. Of course stars close to Earth will look bright, but others are bright because they are giant stars. They also have different colors – red, yellow, and bluish white – showing their different temperatures. The cooler ones are red and the hottest are blue. Our nearest star, the Sun, is an ordinary small, yellow star in the middle of its life. Giant and supergiant stars are hundreds of times larger, and dwarf stars are hundreds of times smaller than the Sun. Unlike the lonely Sun, many stars circle each other in pairs, or are in larger groups of circling stars. Between all these stars gas and dust is spread very thinly through space. Thicker clouds of gas and dust are called nebulae. You can see a nebula if the gas glows or if the dust reflects light from nearby stars. Dark nebulae do not glow, but show up as dark empty patches of sky, because they block the light from the stars behind them.

Little and large
Here you can see the lives of two very different stars. The small one will shine for about 10,000 million years. The giant star will only shine for a few million years.

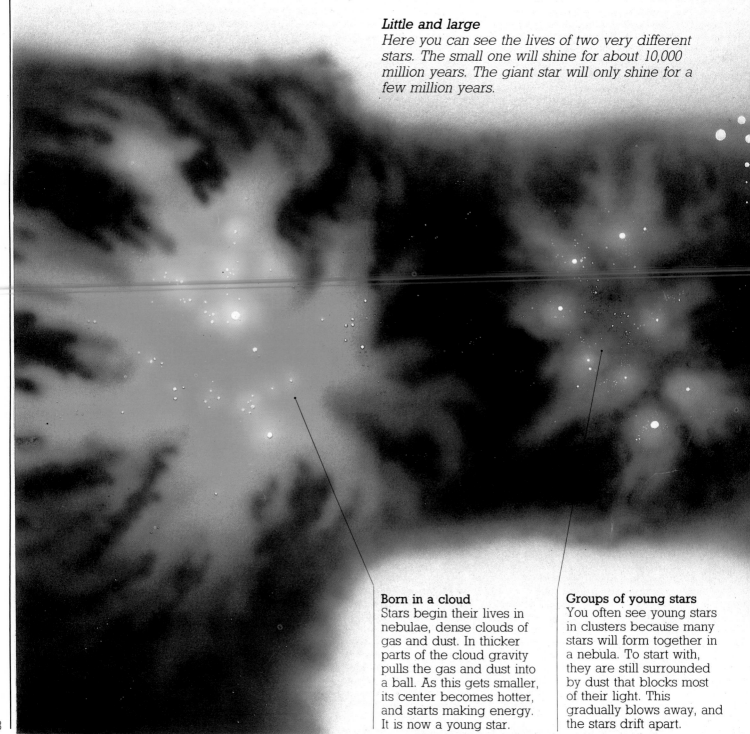

Born in a cloud
Stars begin their lives in nebulae, dense clouds of gas and dust. In thicker parts of the cloud gravity pulls the gas and dust into a ball. As this gets smaller, its center becomes hotter, and starts making energy. It is now a young star.

Groups of young stars
You often see young stars in clusters because many stars will form together in a nebula. To start with, they are still surrounded by dust that blocks most of their light. This gradually blows away, and the stars drift apart.

Stars like the Sun

A star like the Sun uses up its hydrogen gas steadily. It will pour out heat and light for about 10,000 million years until all its gas is used up.

Giant stars

Stars do not all start off the same weight. If a young star is heavier than the Sun, it will make much more energy and use up its hydrogen gas much more quickly. It will shine steadily for only a few million years before it begins to die.

Variable stars

Stars do not all shine steadily like the Sun. Some stars change regularly, getting alternately stronger then weaker every few days or months. They seem to be swelling up and then shrinking. Other stars suddenly flare up very brightly then gradually fade again. All stars that change like this are called variable stars.

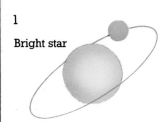

1

Bright star

2

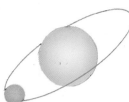

Fainter star

1

White dwarf star

2

Explosion of gases round white dwarf star

Binary stars

Some stars that seem to get brighter regularly are really two stars circling each other, though they look like one star. They are brightest when you can see them both. When one is in front of the other it blocks out the light from the star behind it.

New stars (novae)

These are not really new stars, just faint stars that suddenly flare up brightly, then gradually dim. If a pair of stars contains a white dwarf, it may pull gas from its companion. The extra gas would explode and it would look like a new star from Earth.

The death of a star

Stars do not go on shining steadily forever. When the hydrogen gas in the center is used up, the star can no longer make energy, but this does not mean it fades away. Some stars end their lives very violently in a huge explosion.

Red giants

At the end of their lives all stars swell up into red giant or supergiant stars. When the Sun becomes a red giant it will be so big that it will swallow up Mercury, Venus, and Earth. This will happen in about 5,000 million years' time.

A glowing shell

As the red giant expands, the center of the star gets smaller. The outer layers of the star keep moving outward, making a glowing shell of gas called a planetary nebula. All that remains of the star is its central core.

Recycled stars

When stars disintegrate they join the cloud of gas and dust between the stars. This is so thin that it's really a vacuum. If it collects into thicker clouds, new stars will begin to form, so star material is never wasted.

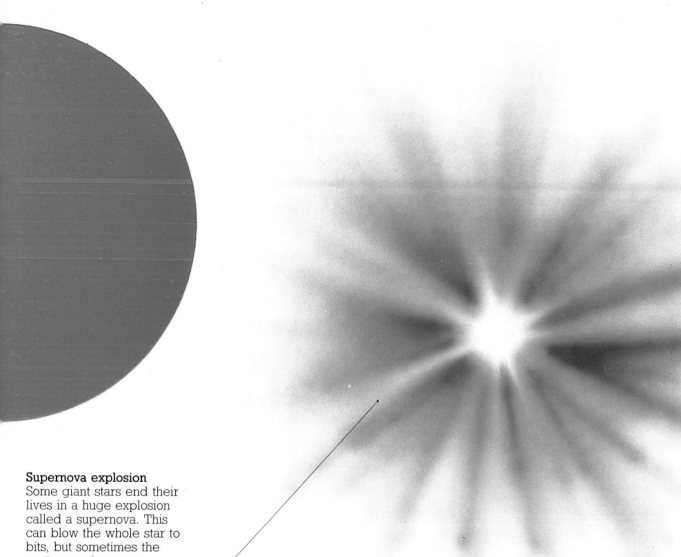

Supernova explosion

Some giant stars end their lives in a huge explosion called a supernova. This can blow the whole star to bits, but sometimes the center survives as a neutron star or a black hole (*see pages 52-53*).

Neutron stars and pulsars

A tiny spinning neutron star may be left after a supernova. Some, called pulsars, send out a narrow beam of radio waves, which sweeps around as the star spins. Like a lighthouse beam, it seems to switch on and off and can only be seen when it points our way.

White dwarf stars

A star like the Sun becomes a white dwarf after losing its outer layers. It does not make any energy, but it continues to shine while it cools down.

BLACK HOLES

Astronomers do not really *know* a lot about the Universe. They can only work out what they think happens, in the life of a star for instance, and then see if their measurements agree with their ideas. Black holes are one idea that is very difficult to check. Astronomers have worked out that when a heavy star has used up all its "fuel" and stops making energy, it will collapse. As the gas is packed tighter and tighter, its gravity gets stronger and stronger. If it is a giant star nothing can stop this collapse, its escape velocity reaches the speed of light, and the star "blacks out." Anything falling in will be trapped forever, because nothing can move faster than light.

Although a black hole cannot actually be seen, there are indications that they may exist. For example, if it is close to a star, its gravity might pull gas from the star. The gas would spiral around the black hole, getting very hot and giving out X rays, which astronomers can detect.

Gas guzzler
In the picture a large star and a black hole are circling around each other. The enormous gravity of the black hole is sucking gas from the star. This whirls around, getting hotter and hotter before disappearing into the black hole.

Other black holes

Nobody knows how many black holes there are. Some astronomers think there may be a black hole at the center of our Galaxy, and in the distant quasars. They could also form in the tight groups of stars called globular clusters.

Cygnus X-1

Cygnus X-1 is a source of X rays coming from a point near a giant star. This star has a companion that cannot be seen through a telescope, and Cygnus X-1 seems to be this companion. It may be a black hole.

Einstein

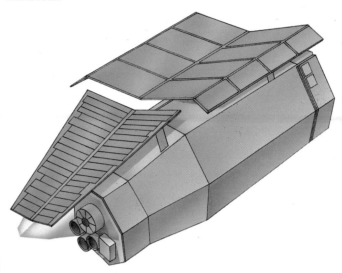

X rays from space cannot travel through our atmosphere so we can only collect them using rockets and satellites. This satellite, called Einstein, studied several sources of X rays, like Cygnus X-1, that could be black holes. It also found X rays coming from the center of a star cluster where there could be a black hole.

INVISIBLE ASTRONOMY

With ordinary telescopes you can see the light from stars and galaxies, but you cannot see the other kinds of radiation they produce, like X rays, radio waves, and ultraviolet and infrared radiation. This radiation carries information that helps astronomers to understand what the Universe is like. With radio waves they can detect huge clouds of gas in space and this has helped them to map the shape of our Galaxy. X rays show astronomers violent activity like supernova explosions, or possibly gas disappearing into black holes. With infrared radiation they can "see" young stars forming. Ultraviolet light comes from the very hottest stars.

However, our atmosphere stops a lot of this radiation from reaching the Earth. Telescopes on the ground can only collect light, radio waves, and some infrared radiation. The rest must be collected above the Earth's atmosphere by rockets or satellites. Information from satellites is made into pictures by computers, which often add bright colors to make the pictures clearer and easier to understand.

Pictures from space
Each of these pictures was produced using a different kind of invisible radiation. You can compare them with the small pictures (inset) taken using ordinary light. The radio picture came from a radio telescope on Earth, but the others were all produced by spacecraft.

Using radio waves
The radio telescope picture (left) shows the center of our Galaxy; the strongest signals are red and the weakest blue. An ordinary telescope cannot penetrate the center of the Galaxy – it only shows the stars nearer to us.

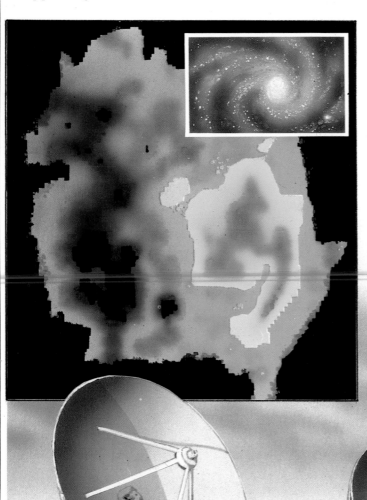

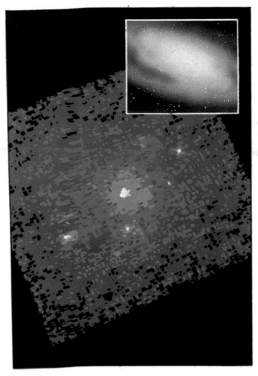

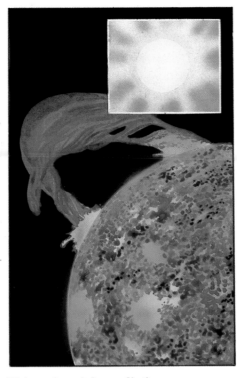

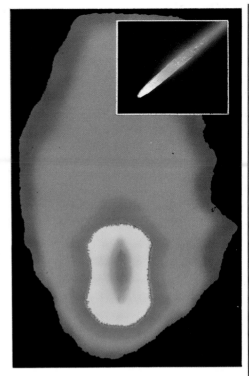

Using X rays
This X ray picture of the Andromeda Galaxy was produced by the Einstein Observatory satellite. The bright spots show where X rays are coming from. The strongest X rays are in the brightest spot at the center.

Using ultraviolet radiation
An ultraviolet telescope on the Skylab space station produced this picture of the Sun. The huge prominence would be very difficult to see from Earth because the ordinary light from the Sun is so powerful.

Using infrared radiation
The InfraRed Astronomical Satellite discovered this comet. The picture shows the cloud of gas and dust around the comet. The red area is brightest, while the cooler, blue part stretches out as the comet's tail.

Radio telescopes
A radio telescope collects radio waves using a curved dish. Astronomers need large radio telescopes to make accurate pictures, so they use several smaller telescopes together, acting like one large one. In the Very Large Array shown below there are 27 dishes. Together, they are as accurate as a single radio telescope 21 miles (34km) across.

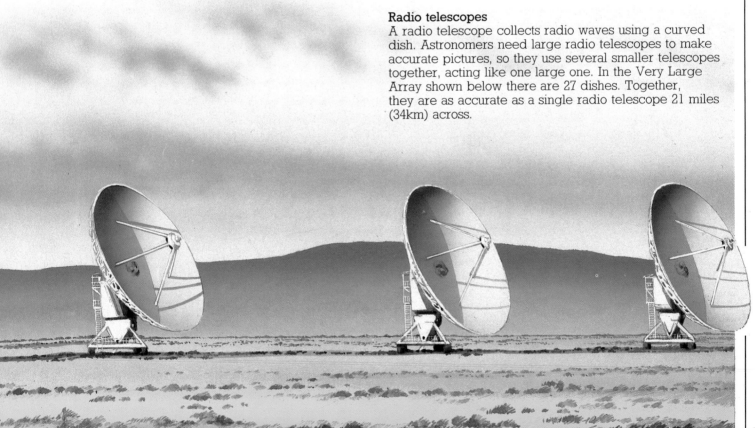

GALAXIES OF STARS

The stars you see in the night sky are part of a gigantic family of stars, called the Galaxy. There may be as many as 100,000 million stars in the Galaxy, but you cannot see them all. Our star, the Sun, is near the edge, and when you look toward the center you see light from other stars and nebulae. This is the Milky Way, a faint band that you can see across the sky on clear nights. The center of it is hidden by dusty clouds.

Astronomers have worked out what our Galaxy is like by looking at other galaxies and by measuring the movements of gas clouds between the stars. It is a flat spiral about 100,000 light years across, with two "arms" winding around a bright bulge at the center. The arms contain nebulae where new stars are born. The Sun is in one of these arms. Around the edge of the Galaxy are about 200 groups of perhaps 100,000 older stars. Our Galaxy is not alone. There are about 100,000 million other galaxies all over the Universe.

Our spiral home

Earth is in a spiral galaxy like this. It's nearest neighbors are two smaller galaxies, called the Magellanic Clouds. They are in a group of about 20 galaxies including the Andromeda Spiral. This group is in a larger cluster with many other groups of galaxies.

Galaxy shapes

Galaxies come in different shapes and sizes but there are three main types. Elliptical galaxies contain mostly older stars. A barred spiral galaxy has a bar through its center with "arms" at each end of the bar. An irregular galaxy has no definite shape, but has a lot of dust and bright nebulae.

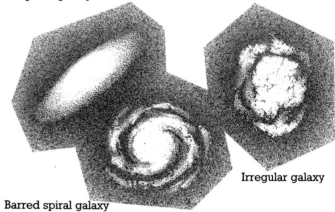

Elliptical galaxy

Irregular galaxy

Barred spiral galaxy

Our Solar System

X

Spinning spirals

Our Galaxy spins around, but the center moves faster than the edge. The Sun takes about 300 million years to travel once round the Galaxy, moving 137 miles (220km) every second.

Active galaxies

These galaxies produce much more energy than ordinary ones, but nobody knows why. Some have extremely bright centers while in others some kind of explosion seems to have taken place.

Quasars

Quasars may be very young galaxies. They look like stars, but seem further away, smaller, and brighter than most galaxies. Nobody knows how such a small object can produce so much energy.

Colliding galaxies

Sometimes galaxies may get too close to each other, but this does not cause a huge crash in space. They pull each other out of shape, or a larger galaxy may gradually swallow up a smaller one.

STARTING WITH A BANG

When astronomers look out into space, far beyond our Galaxy, they see many other galaxies in all directions. These distant galaxies all seem to be moving away from us and from each other, and those furthest away are moving the fastest. So we seem to be in an expanding universe, but what happened to start this expansion?

Astronomers think that about 20,000 million years ago all the material in the Universe was sent flying outward in all directions. They cannot explain how or why this happened but they compare it with a massive explosion and call it the Big Bang. At first the universe was very, very hot, but it cooled as it expanded and became the universe we know today.

The distant galaxies are so far away that the light from them takes a long time to reach us. Astronomers can see faint galaxies 10,000 million light years away. This means that the light from these galaxies has taken 10,000 million years to reach us, so we see them as they were 10,000 million years ago, and we do not know what these galaxies are really like today. As you look out into space you are also looking back in time.

Remains of the Big Bang
If the Big Bang happened it would have left weak radio waves all through space. In 1965 background radiation was discovered coming from all directions. This does not prove the theory, but is an important clue.

The Big Bang
Just after the Big Bang, the Universe was so hot that astronomers call it a fireball. As it expanded in all directions, it cooled and the gases hydrogen and helium were formed. These gases then turned into galaxies, which continued to rush away from each other.

The expanding universe
If you draw spots all over a balloon and then blow it up, you will see for yourself how the Universe is expanding. Imagine each dot is a galaxy. As you blow the balloon up, each dot, or galaxy, moves further away from all the others. It doesn't matter which galaxy you are in, the others are all moving away from you and those furthest away are moving the fastest of all.

How big is the Universe?
The most distant things
astronomers can see are
quasars, and the furthest
of these seems to be about
13,000 million light years
away. They do not know
what is beyond this so they
cannot tell how big the
Universe is.

Will it ever stop expanding?
The Universe may go on
expanding forever, but if
the pull of gravity between
the galaxies is strong
enough they will start
moving inward. If they
eventually meet, there may
be another Big Bang.

OUR FUTURE IN SPACE

In the future the energy we use on Earth could be supplied by solar-powered satellites. These would collect the constant energy from the Sun and beam it down to Earth to be used as electricity. The satellites would be gigantic, maybe 6.2 miles (10km) long and 3.1 miles (5km) wide, so they would have to be built in space. At first all the satellite parts would be brought up from Earth, but in the future it will be cheaper to produce them in space. There would be a base on the Moon for mining engineers and factories in space to produce the building materials from the Moon rock. The space engineers would live in a space station that would be large enough to spin without making them dizzy. This would press them against the outer edge (the floor) and they would have a feeling of weight, as on Earth. There would also be day and night to make it as like Earth as possible. Later there could be space colonies where millions of people would be born and live the whole of their lives, only visiting Earth as tourists.

A picture of the future?
The huge spinning wheel is a home in space for thousands of people. Some of them are aboard the starship preparing for their long journey to another planet, circling a distant star. Other passengers are arriving by shuttle spacecraft from the planet below.

Energy from the Sun
Solar-powered satellites will turn sunlight into electricity and beam it down to Earth as radio waves. Huge receivers about 6 miles (10km) across will change the radio waves back into electricity for us to use.

Space materials
Future space builders will mine the asteroids as well as the Moon because it is cheaper than mining the Earth. Space tugs would tow small asteroids near to the Earth, and space factories would use the asteroid material.

Space colonies
You would feel quite at home in a space colony, even though it would simply be a huge spinning cylinder. There would be buildings and landscapes, just like Earth's. The weather would be fine and normal food would be grown there.

Starships
It would take thousands of years for the spacecraft we have at the moment to get to the nearest star. However, scientists are working on new forms of propulsion to drive probes at much higher speeds. Even so, journeys to the stars will be very long.

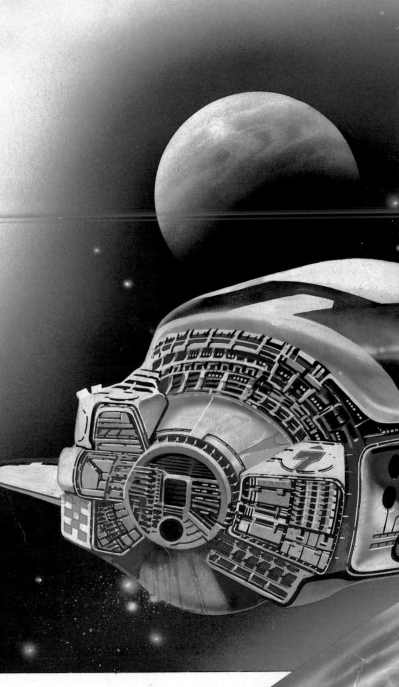

Are we alone?
Nobody knows if there is life elsewhere in the Universe. There may be planets circling other stars but we cannot see them. Radio messages have been sent out toward stars but they will take about 25,000 years to reach them.

Making a planet like Earth
A scientist has suggested that Venus could be made more like Earth by putting plants into the atmosphere. These would change the suffocating carbon dioxide into oxygen, then humans could live safely on the cooler parts of Venus.

Living on other planets
On most other planets, like Mars, or on the Moon, human beings would live inside protective domes. These would hold the air they need to breathe and protect them from any harmful radiation. Outside the domes they would have to wear a space suit.

61

MAPS OF THE SKY

The patterns that the stars make in the sky are called constellations. On these pages you can see maps of the constellations. In the center of the maps are the stars that would be overhead if you were standing at the North Pole (left) or at the South Pole (right). The central stars are the easiest to find. Toward the edge of each map are the stars that are nearer the horizon. The best way to find your way around the constellations is to look for the shape of a familiar one and try to find others in relation to that one.

The Earth is spinning all the time, so the constellations seem to move across the sky from east to west. This means that to use these maps you will have to turn them around until they match what you can see in the sky.

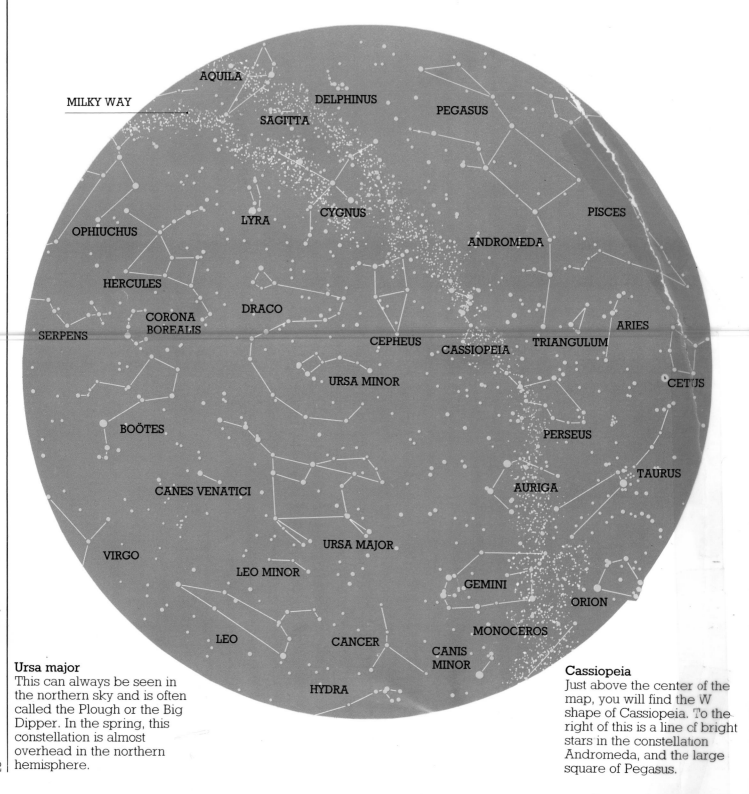

MILKY WAY

AQUILA
DELPHINUS
PEGASUS
SAGITTA
CYGNUS
PISCES
LYRA
OPHIUCHUS
ANDROMEDA
HERCULES
DRACO
ARIES
CORONA
BOREALIS
SERPENS
CEPHEUS
TRIANGULUM
CASSIOPEIA
CETUS
URSA MINOR
BOÖTES
PERSEUS
CANES VENATICI
TAURUS
AURIGA
VIRGO
URSA MAJOR
LEO MINOR
GEMINI
ORION
LEO
CANCER
MONOCEROS
CANIS
MINOR
HYDRA

Ursa major
This can always be seen in the northern sky and is often called the Plough or the Big Dipper. In the spring, this constellation is almost overhead in the northern hemisphere.

Cassiopeia
Just above the center of the map, you will find the W shape of Cassiopeia. To the right of this is a line of bright stars in the constellation Andromeda, and the large square of Pegasus.

The northern and southern skies
The constellations near the centers of these maps can only be seen from one half of the Earth (north on the left and south on the right). Some others, shown near the edges of the maps, appear in the north in winter and the south in summer, or the other way around.

Orion's belt
Look along the line of Orion's belt and you will find Sirius, the brightest star in the sky. In the other direction is the beautiful cluster of young stars, the Pleiades, beyond the red giant, Aldebaran.

Orion
Orion's "belt" of three bright stars is easy to find in the north in winter and the south in summer. In the opposite corners of Orion are two supergiant stars – Rigel, which is blue, and Betelgeuse, which is red.

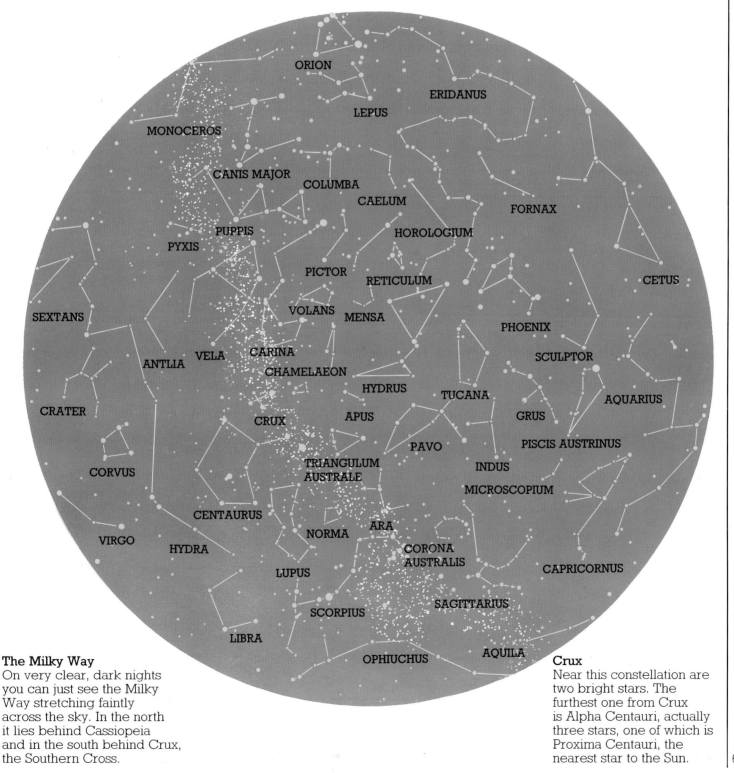

The Milky Way
On very clear, dark nights you can just see the Milky Way stretching faintly across the sky. In the north it lies behind Cassiopeia and in the south behind Crux, the Southern Cross.

Crux
Near this constellation are two bright stars. The furthest one from Crux is Alpha Centauri, actually three stars, one of which is Proxima Centauri, the nearest star to the Sun.

63

INDEX

Acknowledgements
Dorling Kindersley would like to thank Sandra Archer and Lynn
Bresler for their help in producing this book.